D1247143

FOCUS ON THE FAMILY®

TONY EVANS
KINGDOM
STEWARDSHIP

MANAGING ALL OF LIFE
UNDER GOD'S RULE

TYNDALE

Tyndale House Publishers
Carol Stream, Illinois

Kingdom Stewardship: Managing All of Life under God's Rule
© 2020 Tony Evans. All rights reserved.

A Focus on the Family book published by Tyndale House Publishers, Carol Stream, Illinois 60188

Focus on the Family and the accompanying logo and design are federally registered trademarks of Focus on the Family, 8605 Explorer Drive, Colorado Springs, CO 80920.

TYNDALE and Tyndale's quill logo are registered trademarks of Tyndale House Publishers.

Portions of chapter 3 have been adapted from EXPERIENCING GOD TOGETHER, copyright © 2015 Tony Evans. Published by Harvest House Publishers, Eugene, OR, 97408. www.harvesthousepublishers.com.

Portions of chapter 11 have been adapted from *Living in Financial Victory* by Tony Evans (Chicago: Moody Publishers, 2013). Used by permission.

All Scripture quotations, unless otherwise indicated, are taken from the *New American Standard Bible*®. Copyright © 1960, 1962, 1963, 1968, 1971, 1972, 1973, 1975, 1977, 1995 by The Lockman Foundation. Used by permission. (www.Lockman.org).

Scripture quotations marked (esv) are taken from *The Holy Bible, English Standard Version*. Copyright © 2001 by CrosswayBibles, a publishing ministry of Good News Publishers. Used by permission. All rights reserved.

Scripture quotations marked (niv) are taken from the *Holy Bible, New International Version*®, *NIV*®. Copyright © 1973, 1978, 1984, 2011 by Biblica, Inc.® Used by permission of Zondervan. All rights reserved worldwide. (*www.zondervan.com*) The "NIV" and "New International Version" are trademarks registered in the United States Patent and Trademark Office by Biblica, Inc.®

Cover design by Sally Dunn

Cover image: iStockphoto//PeopleImages

For information about special discounts for bulk purchases, please contact Tyndale House Publishers at csresponse@tyndale.com, or call 1-800-323-9400.

Library of Congress Control Number: 2019949732

ISBN 978-1-58997-953-6

Printed in the United States of America

26   25   24   23   22   21   20
7   6   5   4   3   2   1

This work is gratefully dedicated to my good friends Mark and Marty Schupbach for their personal friendship, ministry support, and passion for biblical stewardship that have encouraged me both personally and professionally.

CONTENTS

INTRODUCTION

Many years ago, during the days of the Wild West, a man robbed a bank in Texas and then fled across the border to Mexico. Chased by a sheriff from Texas, he was finally cornered in an old bar where he thought he'd escape notice. The problem for the sheriff, though, was that the bank robber spoke only Spanish and the sheriff spoke only English. So they had to locate a translator.

Once a translator was found, the sheriff interrogated the bank robber about his stash. For starters, the sheriff asked him where he hid the money. The bank robber replied that he wouldn't tell. The sheriff began to push harder and demanded that the robber tell him where he hid the money. But the bank robber held his ground and told him nothing. Then the sheriff instructed the translator to tell the robber, "If you don't tell me where you stashed the money, I'm going to shoot you right here and right now."

The bank robber saw the seriousness in the sheriff's eyes. He knew he was out of the jurisdiction of American law and that the sheriff could make good on his threat. So the thief told the translator exactly where he hid the money. It was buried beneath an oak tree outside of a nearby barn about two feet under the ground.

When the sheriff pushed the translator to tell him what the bank robber just said, though, the translator changed the story. "He said he ain't tellin' you nothin'!"

Of course that wasn't the truth. But the translator now knew where the stash was hidden!

Communication can be a rough thing. You don't always know when someone is telling you the truth or whether you are getting the full story. When it comes to the area of kingdom stewardship, there is a lot spoken and written on the subject. But a lot of that information is plain wrong or incomplete. Many people simply focus on stewarding money and assume that's all there is to living as a kingdom steward. But money is only one part of your role of managing all you have under God. Biblical stewardship involves more than money. How you choose to spend your time, where you choose to let your thoughts linger, what you choose to say, and how you leverage your position and maximize your talents all have a far greater impact on the outcomes of your life. Yes, stewardship includes money, but the true treasures of this topic also include so much more.

It is my goal in this book to communicate a practical theology of stewardship that connects it to the broader theme and worldview of the kingdom agenda. The kingdom agenda *is the visible manifestation of the comprehensive rule of God over every area of life*. Only when stewardship is seen against the backdrop of this broader kingdom worldview where all of life is lived under God's rule can we fully understand, appreciate, and benefit from the managerial responsibility God has entrusted to us as His kingdom stewards.

PART I

THE FOUNDATION OF KINGDOM STEWARDSHIP

1

MEANING

During my years in seminary, money came to us as a family fairly infrequently. My wife, Lois, stayed home with the children, and I worked what jobs I could while also going to school full-time. To describe that season as one of near financial destitution would not be an exaggeration. Anyone who has attended seminary or graduate school with a spouse and children to care for will understand. Surviving became the goal. Eating became the goal. Keeping the car running and the electricity on became the goal. We aimed to reach these goals each week through as many strategies as we could.

One of the ways we sought a source of income came through house-sitting for families who traveled on vacations or business trips. The seminary I attended had developed strong relationships with many wealthy families in Dallas, nurturing a trust that would open the door for such work. These families assumed (and rightly so) that the seminary students who house-sat for them would not steal from them. They also assumed that their children would be properly looked after, their animals cared for, and their valuables protected. And what valuables they were! Some of these families had cars that cost more than most houses!

Now, you can imagine how excited Lois and I were each time we were chosen to house-sit for a family. Not only were we assured that we would be eating well all week long, but we also got to live it up in palaces while driving fancy cars. To top it off, we got paid to do this. Moving on up from our tiny apartment to an enormous home, finely decorated inside and with a well-manicured lawn outside, brought us great joy. One time I even got to drive a Bentley to school. Yes, I took the longest route possible.

However, despite our enthusiasm for our increase in living standards, we needed to stay realistic in our thinking. Lois would often remind me by saying, "Tony, this is not your house." She would say this because, at times, I would get a little too comfortable with my surroundings rather than remember that the family had merely left us in charge during their absence.

I'll admit—it is easy to get comfortable and forget what is yours and what is not yours when you are in the vicinity of something or even someone. Proximity paints unrealistic pictures of power and possession in all of our minds. Just because we had been tasked with managing a property for a weekend or a week, this did not make us the owners of that property. We were asked to manage the premises of another. Our role involved overseeing the well-being of what was not ours at all.

The life lessons learned during this time in our young lives have stayed with me in a profoundly spiritual way. This wasn't because of any book I read or study I did, but because I experienced firsthand what stewardship really looks like. At the end of our stay, we left the homes in as good a shape—if not better—as when we arrived. We left the food (if there was any left over). We left the cars. We left the kids we were child-sitting, furniture, pets, lawn, sound systems, and large-screen TVs. We left it all. Didn't take one single thing with us. Why? Because it was not ours to take. It had been ours to manage only. We had been entrusted as stewards.

Recently I experienced a year shadowed by a significant amount of loss. I lost friends and family members to illnesses and even suicide. It seemed like each new month brought about the devastating news of another person's passing. While this season was tough, it also served as a wake-up call and healthy reminder that we take nothing with us when we head home into glory. None of the things we buy. None of the things we treasure. None of the things we save up for or invest our time and talents in. The only things that get sent on to heaven are the things we did for God and for others through His power and presence in us. These are things with eternal impact.

Many people talk about "legacy" when someone leaves this earth. Legacy simply refers to what a person has left behind. But the true legacy involves that which is sent ahead. We will never fully know our personal legacies until we stand before our Savior and hear Him say, "Well done, My good and faithful servant."

> *We will never fully know our personal legacies until we stand before our Savior and hear Him say, "Well done, My good and faithful servant."*

Until then, we have been charged with the task of managing what He has given us on earth. We have been asked to fill in the context of that "well done" we hope He will one day say to us. This responsibility is called stewardship. It is a managerial role, not an ownership position.

God's House

In football, you will often read or hear the phrase "This is our house" or "Defend the house!" What this means is that when a visiting team comes to play, the home team makes it known that the visitors have entered into their domain. The home team makes it clear that they plan to protect, defend, and rule their house. The goal is to send the visiting team back to their own house with a defeat.

While sayings like that in sports can often be chalked up to mere hype (after all, many home teams lose games in "their house"), when

God makes a similar claim to His own creation—He speaks seriously. Psalm 24:1 states it clearly, "The earth is the Lord's, and all it contains, the world, and those who dwell in it." God claims comprehensive kingdom ownership over all creation. This is His house. This is His kingdom. We live in His domain.

Psalm 89:11 puts it this way, "The heavens are Yours, the earth also is Yours; the world and all it contains, You have founded them."

Revelation 4:11 states, "Worthy are You, our Lord and our God, to receive glory and honor and power; for You created all things, and because of Your will they existed, and were created."

> *God owns it all. And since God owns it all, neither you nor I have any right to claim ownership of something that is not ours.*

God owns it all. And since God owns it all, neither you nor I have any right to claim ownership of something that is not ours. Even if we did make that claim, it wouldn't make any real difference just as it wouldn't make any real difference if I claimed that any of the houses we watched during seminary were mine. When the true owners returned, I'd be kicked to the curb and undoubtedly I wouldn't even receive the payment that was due me for house-sitting. No owner is going to stand by while someone else seeks to take what is theirs.

Neither will God stand by as His creatures seek to usurp His sovereignty and role as the rightful owner of all of creation.

There is no shared ownership in God's kingdom.

There are no partnerships or additional signatories on any deeds or titles.

God owns it all.

Once you clearly understand and apply that spiritual truth to your life, you have set yourself on a journey of understanding as well as a pathway of unleashing your fullest potential. Most people never get this. Most people never choose to live by this principle. They think or act as if they own what they really don't own, simply because they have it. Yet what God has established in His divine order of creation is a management-based created order. Businesses have entered into a new trend over the last few years, having identified the large financial waste and inefficiency of having upper-level executive roles. We are seeing fewer companies and nonprofits seeking to fill executive director, C-suite, or top-leadership roles. Escalating budgets at that level, as well as a lack of accountability related to outward-facing work assignments for these types of positions, have encouraged the trend to what is now known as the "self-managed workplace."

A self-managed workplace consists of high-performing management personnel who report to no one other than each other and the owner, president, or board of directors. These teams require a significant amount of self-awareness, trust, and cohesion among the directors, but when they do have these things, they have demonstrated a greater ability to perform efficiently, productively, and at a lower cost to the business or non-profit.

There are dangers to running a business in this manner, but those dangers run high only when personal responsibility runs low. As long as each person adequately and authentically manages his or her work, communicates well, and respects the goals and processes of other teams, this style of leadership propels financial growth, boosts company morale, and fosters a culture of connectivity.

Forbes recently published findings on this trend toward self-management: "To be effective in this new world, everyone, in his or her own way, will need to assume a leadership role."[1] I'm sure they weren't intending to make a spiritual statement, but that is a very spiritual statement when looked at in the context of kingdom stewardship.

Forbes was saying that when each person properly stewards his or her time, talents, and resources in a way that reflects a spirit of responsibility, enthusiasm, excellence, and drive—the organization grows. A management style that commissions a heart of leadership throughout the organization leads to motivated and productive employees. Similarly, our stewardship in God's economy and creative structure is entirely up to us as well. No human being ultimately rules over us to tell us what we need to do, when we need to do it, and in what manner it should be done. God rules, and through the sacrifice of His Son, God has given us direct access to Himself. In the final analysis, each of us reports directly to God—the President per se. We report to the Trinity—the Board per se. And when we do, we discover that He has entrusted us with the freedom, responsibility, and opportunity to manage all within our domain.

— ❧ —

God's trust in you can inspire you to make the most of what He's placed within your disposal.

— ❧ —

What you do with the time, talents, and treasures God has given you is up to you. The choices you make. The decisions on how you spend your days. The focus of your mind. Even the thoughts you think. That is all up to you. And because it is up to you, you have a unique ability to directly influence the rate of your own spiritual progress.

That reality ought to invigorate you to work harder, seek creative ways to grow, and look for how you can fully maximize all that God has given to you. God's trust in you can inspire you to make the most of what He's placed within your disposal.

God's Creation

Owners of property often hire management companies to manage the property for them. God has a management company for His creation—it's called humanity. One of the primary reasons the Lord created humanity was to manage what He owns.

Before God created humanity, He had another management company: the angels. The angels had been positioned to manage God's property. However, one angel chose to go rogue, and with his own rebellion, to draw a significant number of other angels into the rebellion with him. Isaiah 14:12-15 recounts this scenario for us:

> How you have fallen from heaven, O star of the morning, son of the dawn! You have been cut down to the earth, you who have weakened the nations! But you said in your heart, "I will ascend to heaven; I will raise my throne above the stars of God, and I will sit on the mount of assembly in the recesses of the north. I will ascend above the heights of the clouds; I will make myself like the Most High." Nevertheless you will be thrust down to Sheol, to the recesses of the pit.

Lucifer rebelled against God and tried to establish ownership on God's premises. He sought to enact a joint venture with other angels, and as a result, led a third of all angels into a cosmic kingdom rebellion (Revelation 12:4). This rebellion was hugely unsuccessful, as Jesus tells us in Luke 10:18, "I was watching Satan fall from heaven like lightning." The so-called shining one left a streak of shame across the sky as he tumbled to his eternal demise.

Satan, who got a name-change from Lucifer as a result of his rebellion, was kicked out of heaven down to the third planet from the sun. That's why when you open your Bibles to read about the beginning of known time, you will see that the earth was without form. Void and darkness was upon the face of the deep, so God had to create light when He created mankind. God had to separate the land from the water when He initiated the existence of the world. He carried out a major reconstruction when He brought humanity into existence. But prior to our creation, Satan lived in swampy, dark, and damp disarray until the time when a new group of managers were assigned.

Enter Adam.

Psalm 8:3-8 describes Adam's role, and subsequently our roles as well. We read,

> When I consider Your heavens, the work of Your fingers, the moon and the stars, which You have ordained; what is man that You take thought of him, and the son of man that You care for him? Yet You have made him a little lower than God, and You crown him with glory and majesty! You make him to rule over the works of Your hands; You have put all things under his feet, all sheep and oxen, and also the beasts of the field, the birds of the heavens and the fish of the sea, whatever passes through the paths of the seas.

Humanity has been placed a little lower than the angels—we are constitutionally inferior, for example, because we can't disappear, fly around, or think with angelic intellect. Yet God has still crowned humanity with majesty and has given us the task of looking after His creation. That's stewardship. That's management. We report to God Himself as we carry out the managerial roles of stewarding His resources. God's goal in creating man was to demonstrate what He could do in and through an inferior being (man) that was dependent upon Him rather than a superior being (Satan) that was in rebellion against Him.

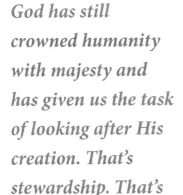

God has still crowned humanity with majesty and has given us the task of looking after His creation. That's stewardship. That's management.

The definition of kingdom stewardship is *the divinely authorized responsibility for believers to faithfully oversee the protection and expansion*

of the assets (time, talents, and treasures) God has entrusted to them to manage on His behalf.

Thus, kingdom stewards can be defined as *believers who faithfully oversee the protection and expansion of the assets God has entrusted to them to manage on His behalf.*

Stewardship always involves both protecting and expanding the assets of another. A kingdom steward protects and expands God's creation on His behalf because He is the King. Creation is His kingdom and we are His managing crew. This is similar to how a bank's role is not only to protect a person's valuables and assets, but also to grow them through interest on deposits. A steward doesn't merely guard another's assets. A proper steward grows them.

Once you learn to identify yourself as a manager over everything that God puts in your hand, it changes how you look at everything around you.

Once you learn to identify yourself as a manager over everything that God puts in your hand, it changes how you look at everything around you. God created mankind to be His stewards, and a steward is to manage things according to the intention and vision of the owner. God made each of us in His image. When we do things that oppose His will, there's going to be conflict. This is similar to what happens in any workplace. The managers work for the owner. The owner does not work for the managers. We have been created in God's image. Thankfully, He has not been made in ours.

When you woke up this morning and stood before a mirror, you saw you. If you lifted up your right hand, you saw your right hand in the mirror. All the mirror did was bounce back to you your image. The image in the mirror follows the movements of whatever it is reflecting. Thus, as God chose to make humanity in His image, His intention was for us to mirror His movement and nature in the visible realm as part of His management team over things that humanity does not own but has been tasked to steward.

When God had created the earth and prepared it for humanity, we read over and over that God saw it and said that it is "good." He was well pleased with what He made. Then after He made man, He was so pleased that He even rested. He knew that His creation could and would sustain itself at a minimum, and if stewarded well by humans, it could produce a society capable of building and enjoying great success and productivity. God had made a world where we would never run out of air, foliage, or space. He packed so much into our creation that we have not yet even discovered it all—this after thousands of years of exploration.

Every idea, invention, and imaginative blend of design has been initiated in that which God has already made.

Our job as stewards over His creation does not depend on our ability to produce things out of nothing. Rather, we are to successfully uncover ways to utilize and advance the resources already made. Every idea, invention, and imaginative blend of design has been initiated in that which God has already made. As 1 Corinthians 4:7 says, "For who regards you as superior? What do you have that you did not receive? And if you did receive it, why do you boast as if you had not received it?"

Nothing you nor I have ever thought of or made originated from us. We had to piggyback off of something God made first. We eat because God created vegetation and animals. We wear clothing because God created the materials from which clothes are sewn. We build houses because God created trees and metals that form the elements we combine into structures. Everything we have has been borrowed from our one, true Source—God Himself.

We are never tasked with creating something out of nothing. Our role is to cultivate, keep, defend, and expand that which God has given us (Genesis 2:15). God placed Adam in the garden called Eden and instructed him to bear the responsibility of cultivating it. This was Adam's homestead. He was told that he could eat from anything in the garden, except for the tree of the knowledge of good and evil. An immense amount of freedom was placed in his hands to unlock the potential of the home he had been given. Shortly thereafter, Eve joined him in the task of unleashing the full potential of their shared domain.

The Freedom God Gives

Many people don't see the freedom given to us in the garden. For whatever reason, perhaps because of our sin nature as Paul describes in Romans 7:7-8, we focus on the limitations of the single tree in the garden—the one which Adam was told not to eat from. Yet when God placed humanity on earth, He freely bestowed upon mankind the ability to enjoy and expand the various resources at our disposal as we unpack earth's potential.

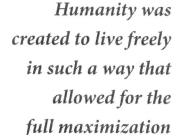

Humanity was created to live freely in such a way that allowed for the full maximization of their potential under God's rule.

God even charged Adam to maximize the potential of the garden within the sphere of stewardship given to him. Like a parent on Christmas morning, God may have watched with eager anticipation as Adam and Eve went about His creation, seeing what was wrapped and hidden within every crevice, river, plant, and mineral He had made. God wanted Adam and Eve, as well as those who followed after, to access the full benefits of what He made.

In fact, the first governing use of the word "free" is not in the American Constitution. The first governing use of "free" is in the Garden of Eden, given by God Himself. Humanity was created to live freely in such a way that allowed for the full maximization of their potential under God's rule.

Now, true, there was that one tree placed in the center of the garden. This is the tree they were instructed not to eat from. But that was it. Everything else was at their free disposal. Yet despite everything else around them, it was the one tree that brought them down. Why would God put a tree in the middle of the garden—a tree that would bring about death? Because every time they passed this tree, it served as a reminder that this was not their house. They were not the owners of this domain. If it had been their house, Adam and Eve would have made the rules. But only an owner has the authority to hand out rules. Thus, they were to manage everything, but like managers in business who need to stay within an approved budget, their decisions were not theirs to make independently of the owner.

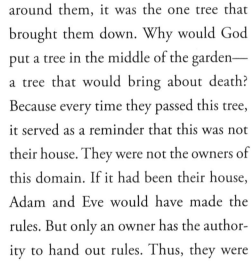

As His managers, He asks us to live by divine revelation and not through human reason.

This tree served as a reminder that God was allowing Adam and Eve to live there—like a parent may allow an adult child to live at home but says, "My house, my rules." But just because they were allowed to live there, it didn't mean they owned the garden.

Just as Christmas trees in our homes are often placed in central locations such as the den in an effort to remind us of the season we are in, this centrally located tree served a perpetual purpose in God's plan. It was a daily reminder of their subordinate dependency on God. It was an invitation to intimacy with the One who knows all truth.

After all, this was a Google tree. God called it the tree of knowledge of good and evil. It was an information center. It held good information and bad information. Within this tree were the mysteries of creation. It held insights and understandings beyond what Adam and Eve had access to on their own. Why wouldn't someone want to take advantage of a tree like that?

Yet God wanted to make it clear from the start that our basis of knowledge is that which He reveals to us. As His managers, He asks us to live by divine revelation and not through human reason. More information is not always a good thing. Decisions based on logic aren't always the correct decisions in a spiritual environment, which is the nature of the environment we live in.

God didn't want our thoughts to compete with His own. When I was a teenager, I would often tell my dad that I disagreed with him. Yet as soon as I got the words "I think" out of my mouth, he would cut me off right there. "You think?" he'd say, quickly. "I don't remember paying you to think." As the man of the house, it was my father's role to guide and direct. And he did a great job at it.

Our world is in chaos today because people are living their lives based on the Google tree. The Bible calls this "human wisdom" (1 Corinthians 2:13; James 3:15). People are making their choices of right and wrong based on their own ability to reason. They are worshiping education, information, relationships, and reason rather than God. The same tree that plagued Adam and Eve, eventually ushering in their destructive demise, is the same tree that plagues us today. People swear by "their truth," not "THE truth." And, just like Adam and Eve, they are suffering at their own hand. Adam handed the management over to Satan when he chose to disobey God (Luke 4:6). As a result, he lost everything.

God had given Adam so much freedom that He even allowed him

to hand over his freedom to the devil, should he choose to do so. And that's just what he did. Adam messed up the mission with which he had been tasked. Just like Adam, each of us has the freedom—as a steward of God's kingdom resources—to mess up our own gardens, our own families, our own influence, and even our own lives. We are free to manage poorly, just as we are free to manage well. The choice is up to each of us. God will never force anyone to obey Him, believe Him, align under Him, or bow to Him. All of that will come naturally in eternity but for now we each have a choice. We can either choose life or we can choose death (Deuteronomy 30:15-20). We choose our actions. God enacts the consequences of our choices as He chooses. Just as a bank that owns a home does not force the residents to keep it neat and tidy, God gives people freedom to choose how they will manage what He has entrusted to them. But, like a bank, He has the right of foreclosure.

> *Many people have good motives all the while making wrong decisions because they are not functioning in the fashion of a stewarding relationship with God.*

Many people have good motives all the while making wrong decisions because they are not functioning in the fashion of a stewarding relationship with God. They are functioning in a mindset of ownership rather than management. Yet in so doing, they discover they have limited resources or limited wisdom on how to best utilize what has been placed before them.

My grandkids love Legos, as many kids do. One grandson in particular absolutely loves them. He loves to dump out a brand-new box of what seems like a million pieces of Legos and then get to work. Legos don't come already constructed. Sure, there are pictures on the buckets and boxes of what a person can do. But none of it comes premade. You don't buy a house or car or building or spaceship already put together. What you do get are the necessary pieces to make it come together. The whole point is to arrange, or steward, the pieces within your control in such a way that you make something greater than what you originally got.

Our role as stewards is to make this world a better place for each person in it, all the while advancing His kingdom agenda on earth.

God has filled creation with Legos. We live in a world containing all kinds of things that can be mixed, matched, combined, grown, cultivated, and maneuvered to bring about something greater than what we first got. God desires for us to craft things out of His creation. We are to build with the things given to us. Our role as stewards is to make this world a better place for each person in it, all the while advancing His kingdom agenda on earth.

Time, Talents, and Treasures

Kingdom stewardship is our earthly response to God's ownership as declared in Psalm 115:16: "The heavens are the heavens of the Lord, but the earth He has given to the sons of men." In other words, God is up there and we are down here. He is expecting us to manage down here according to the direction He gives from up there. Whether or not we do that is up to each of us. There are three distinct areas down here He's given us to steward. We all have these three things, in varying proportions, which God has placed within our realm to manage. They are time, talents, and treasures.

First, you are to steward your time. Sure, we don't all have the same amount of time. While everyone has the same twenty-four hours in a day, we don't all have access to the same number of days. No one knows the length of time God has ordained for them to live. In fact, our family was reminded of this firsthand through the experience of the loss of my niece, who was only in her late thirties when she experienced sudden heart failure. None of us expected this. She appeared to be in perfect health. Yet God ushered her into glory at that young age.

God makes a lot of promises in His Word, but time is not one of them. None of us are even promised tomorrow (James 4:14). That's why stewarding our time is so critical. We are all living on death row. We do not know when the hour will come that God calls us home. Whether we are young or old by humanity's standards is irrelevant to God. God is not bound by time. We are. And because we are, it's important that we learn how to manage our time well.

Ephesians 5:15-17 puts it this way, "Therefore be careful how you walk, not as unwise men but as wise, making the most of your time, because the days are evil. So then do not be foolish, but understand what the will of the Lord is." In this passage, God tells us plainly to watch out for time. We are to steward our time. We are not to waste it.

As David models for us in Psalm 39:4-6, our theology of time ought to be rooted in the truth of the transient nature of life itself. He says,

> LORD, make me to know my end and what is the extent of my
> days; let me know how transient I am. Behold, You have made my
> days as handbreadths, and my lifetime as nothing in Your sight;
> surely every man at his best is a mere breath. Surely every man
> walks about as a phantom; surely they make an uproar for nothing;
> he amasses riches and does not know who will gather them.

David's prayer ought to be our prayer as well. We are to ask God to help us understand the fleeting nature of life. As he writes, we are but a "mere breath." This ought to inspire us to live with a biblical definition of time.

When the Bible speaks of time, it speaks of a boundary of opportunity. We are to make the most of our time by maximizing the potential contained within it. Every time an opportunity is wasted, time is lost. As kingdom stewards, we have been called to use time, not lose it. One of the primary ways to use time wisely shows up in the passage we just looked at in Ephesians 5. In understanding "what the will of the Lord is," we are able to make decisions regarding the management of our time, which will result in productive gain toward advancing God's kingdom agenda. Time is maximized when it is used to accomplish God's will.

Every time an opportunity is wasted, time is lost. As kingdom stewards, we have been called to use time, not lose it.

As Paul wrote in Acts 20:24, we are to use our time to finish the divine destiny and ministry God has given to us. He said, "But I do not consider my life of any account as dear to myself, so that I may finish my course and the ministry which I received from the Lord Jesus, to testify solemnly of the gospel of the grace of God." You can investigate Paul's point further in 2 Timothy 4:6-8.

Paul's words are what each of us ought to aim to say when we reach the end of our time on earth. To say that you have "finished the course" of God's will for your life is to have stewarded your time well. The dreams God has placed in your heart will not become realities unless you take advantage of the opportunities He gives you in this space of time.

Second, in addition to stewarding our time, each of us has been tasked with managing the talents God has given to us. These are the skills He has bestowed upon you for His purposes. Another term people often use for these is "spiritual gifts." God never gives you a spiritual gift just so you can have it. Whatever He has given to you, whether skills, abilities, talents, or personality traits, He's placed it all within your disposal in order to usher in greater good for others and expanded glory for Him.

The Bible declares that your greatest Christian stewardship is not seen in what you get from God but in what God, through you, can give to others as you serve Him in alignment with your gifts. This can sometimes be tough for people to do because we live in a "me" generation. We live in a culture of selfies and narcissistic promotional ways. Yet God has asked each of us to use that which we've been given not to balloon our own platform or build our own brand, but to advance His kingdom agenda on earth. One of the primary components of that agenda is helping those who are less fortunate than yourself according to the gifts and skills He has given you. Loving God and loving others are the first and second commandments we have been given to carry out as kingdom stewards (see Matthew 22:36-39). This love ought to show up in our feet through what we do to strengthen others through the gifts, abilities, and talents God has given to us.

First Peter 4:8-11 urges us to use our gifts in serving God and others while also reminding us of the boomerang effect that extending love and service can positively have in our lives. We read,

> Above all, keep fervent in your love for one another, because love covers a multitude of sins. Be hospitable to one another without complaint. As each one has received a special gift, employ it in serving one another as good stewards of the manifold grace of God. Whoever speaks, is to do so as one who is speaking the utterances of God; whoever serves is to do so as one who is serving by the strength which God supplies; so that in all things

God may be glorified through Jesus Christ, to whom belongs the glory and dominion forever and ever. Amen.

In all things, God is to be glorified through Jesus Christ by the right management of your talents. After all, it is God who has allowed you to receive an education, develop skills, acquire talents, and benefit from them yourself as well. Functioning from a mindset of gratitude for His abundant grace will keep you in alignment with His calling of service with regard to your talents.

Whether it is your home, vehicles, material possessions, or money—God has a purpose for all He has allowed you to obtain in this life.

Third, in addition to your time and your talents, God has given you treasures. This includes not only money but also the tangible items over which you have been assigned as a steward. Whether it is your home, vehicles, material possessions, or money—God has a purpose for all He has allowed you to obtain in this life. That purpose is to serve Him, bring good to others, and expand the manifestation of His kingdom rule on earth.

One way you are to steward stuff, as we often refer to our things, is by bringing it underneath God's sovereignty. The use of what you own must yield to His will. Even owning what you own must yield to His will. As Jesus said in Luke 14:33, "So then, none of you can be My disciple who does not give up all his own possessions." That's not a verse you hear preached on frequently or find as the title of a best-selling book. Can you imagine what would happen if someone published a book called *Follow Jesus by Giving Up All You Own*? It's doubtful that book would get much exposure around the digital world or any buyers at all. Truth be told, we like our stuff. We work for our stuff. We over-extend ourselves at times to get more stuff. What's more, once our stuff loses its newness, we get rid of it or put it into rented storage in order to make room for more stuff. But a kingdom steward must maintain a biblical perspective when it comes to stuff. And that perspective means returning the ownership of all your possessions to God.

No amount of contemporary-based spiritualization can change this truth. Jesus said to give up your stuff. I can hear you now, "But Tony, are you saying that means I shouldn't have a house, or clothes, or money, or a television set?" No, I'm not saying that. The passage isn't saying that. What it does say is that your possessions ought not to possess you.

The problem is not in having stuff. The problem is in possessing it. When what you have carries more weight than what God says, that's a problem. Or when what you have gets more attention than what you give to God, that's a problem. When your decisions are dictated by the accumulation or use of stuff over what God desires for you to do, you are possessed by your possessions. If losing stuff causes more sorrow than losing time with God, you have a problem.

Treasures must remain under His rule, authority, and righteous prioritization for them to be stewarded rightly.

See, everyone reading this book will die with their hands open. You will die empty-handed. Neither you nor I can possess anything in eternity that we had on earth. I'm sure you have never seen a hearse pulling a U-Haul. A biblical perspective on treasures means holding stuff loosely. We cannot hold on to things so tightly that we are bound by the very things themselves. It's not that we can't have things. We just can't be ruled by them. For example, if getting the new car you have your heart set on means sacrificing the responsibilities you have for your family, then that new car is out of alignment with God's ownership of your treasures. God will never lead you to violate His commands in order for you to acquire more things. Treasures must remain under His rule, authority, and righteous prioritization for them to be stewarded rightly. You and I are to possess nothing. Yes, we can use it. But it must never be held on to in such a way that the priority of God in our lives wanes.

As Matthew 6:19-21 urges us,

Do not store up for yourselves treasures on earth, where moth and rust destroy, and where thieves break in and steal. But store up for yourselves treasures in heaven, where neither moth nor rust destroys, and where thieves do not break in or steal; for where your treasure is, there your heart will be also.

Most people actually misunderstand this verse. This verse is not saying to forgo treasures on earth. Rather, it is saying not to lay up treasures on earth. There's a difference. You can have a bank account, house, and more without laying it up in a position of primacy in your heart.

In other words, view and use your treasures with a heart and motivation for eternal rewards in heaven. Invest your treasures on earth for eternal purposes. Glorify God with and through that which He has given to you. Honor Him with your home. Honor Him with your things as well as with your finances. You spiritualize the material by inserting God as the primary focus point and purpose of it.

Managing All of Life under God

As you will see throughout this book, stewardship concerns a lot more than just money, although money is a factor in kingdom stewardship. But stewardship also involves the right management of all your time, all your talents, and all your treasures.

The benefits for managing these three distinct areas include receiving God's manifold blessings. Blessing is the experiencing of God's favor, which He entrusts to us for our benefit as well as for the benefit of others. When you steward well what God has given to you, you set yourself up to be blessed by God. Now, that blessing doesn't always mean getting your wish list or financial abundance. Some of that blessing will be saved for eternity as well. But the blessing will always enable you to manage more, rule more, and expand God's kingdom resources more. As God said in Genesis 1:28, "God blessed them; and God said to them, 'Be fruitful and multiply, and fill the earth, and subdue it; and rule over the fish of the sea and over the birds of the sky and over every living thing that moves on the earth.'" Their blessings were directly tied to and given for the express purpose of ruling God's creation as His kingdom stewards.

— ✿ —

If you want to know the full expression of God working in and through your life, you can do so through learning how to manage well what He has given to you.

— ✿ —

When Adam and Eve blew it, their whole world fell apart and many of their blessings evaporated. Their emotions turned to shambles. Their marriage entered into trouble. Conflict, and even murder, fell upon their home. A battle came into their lives that sought to destroy them. They were removed from the garden in which they had been placed. Not only that, but the whole earth suffered the consequences from their disobedience as thorns, thistles, weeds, pain, and more difficulties became an everyday occurrence in life on earth.

But there are also positive consequences (or rewards) for managing well. God offers both. If you want to know the full expression of God working in and through your life, you can do so through learning how to manage well what He has given to you.

For starters, give up the notion that you own anything at all. This is God's world. He makes the rules. If you want to make the rules, then go create your own world. But until then, you'll need to operate according to His rules. You and I are managers. We are stewards. We have been tasked with maximizing and cultivating all that God has entrusted to us. God does not sell stock in His world. He has not offered up His universe for public ownership. He is not requesting joint ventures. Rather, He is asking each of us to manage things according to His wisdom, by His rules, and with His power. When you do that, you will come to know Him in a more intimate way than ever before because you will get to see Him working in and through your life like never before.

The choice is up to you. Every spiritual blessing has your name on it (Ephesians 1:3). You just need to access each of them through the stewardship choices you make for the praise of His glory and the advancement of His kingdom agenda on earth.

2

MINDSET

Consider how you would feel if you invited a couple to your home for dinner, and they proceeded to go through your entire house and your closets—all on their own. What would you think if one of them started choosing a different outfit to wear from your closet? Or what would you say if they chose to start cooking something different for themselves because they said they didn't like what you made?

You would probably start looking around for a hidden camera or two because you would think that surely this is a prank!

No one goes into another person's house and starts using it as their own.

No one except for every single one of us.

Because that's exactly what we all do to God's house. We claim His creation as our own, giving ourselves free rein to use, misuse, or disregard anything and everything according to our own whims. Yet this is His house and, as such, it comes with His rules, guidelines, design, and intentions. God has made it clear that there is only one owner of His creation, and we are not it. In this earth, you and I own absolutely nothing—including our own lives. As I've had to experience very close to home over the last year or so, God can—and will—take our lives from us when He chooses to do so. We don't own our own timelines. And while we often say that not even tomorrow is promised to us, the truth of the matter is that not even today is promised. Our very moments are held in God's hands.

He owns it all. What's more, He owns *us* all.

God has declared that He created humans to be managers or stewards of what He has entrusted to them. He has also declared that they are never to act as owners or take part in the ownership aspect of His creation. As such, God has called each of us to live as stewards of His kingdom possession. As a reminder, kingdom stewards are believers who faithfully oversee the protection and expansion of the assets God has entrusted to them to manage on His behalf.

We are managers on His behalf, imbued with the responsibility to protect and expand that which has been placed within our personal spheres of influence.

Living life as a kingdom steward is not merely a task; it is a worldview. A worldview is a lens through which you look at all things. Just as a prescription set of glasses made to work with a specific person's eyes will bring into focus that which had previously been out of focus, kingdom stewardship reveals how the world around us truly is. Sin has damaged our spiritual eyes to such a degree that the distortion makes it difficult to navigate through life. Like a blind person dependent upon a cane or canine for assistance, we seek support in many ways. But just as a blind person doesn't receive actual sight from the cane or canine, neither does worldly wisdom give us what we truly need.

> *Living life as a kingdom steward is not merely a task; it is a worldview.*

Only God opens our eyes. Only God restores our sight. It is God who implants in us spiritual eyes to view our lives and the world around us through His lens when we align our worldview in Him. A worldview involves a person's perspective on a matter. To live from a kingdom stewardship worldview includes originating and maintaining all of your thoughts and actions within the grid of God's ownership.

Consequences

Whenever a conflict shows up between His ownership and your attempts at usurping His ownership, negative consequences eventually will arise. That's the result of poor stewardship.

When I preach each Sunday morning, a faithful member of the church prepares and provides my microphone. He's been doing this for years, decades even. His job involves making sure that the microphone works and that it is given to me at the appropriate time to preach. In essence, he stewards the sound of my voice so that it reaches as many people as possible. Now, if he were to one day become confused about his role as a steward and decide that he would like to act as the senior pastor of the church, thus standing up to proclaim his own message on a Sunday morning—there would be consequences. These consequences would undoubtedly arise from the congregation itself in that very moment of time. But there would also be long-term consequences due to a break of trust in the role of stewarding something critical to our church's ministry.

Not much is said about consequences in the day and age in which we live. The focus has shifted to freedoms and each person discovering his or her own version of "truth." However, just because the concept of spiritual, physical, emotional, and relational consequences is often downplayed in our contemporary culture doesn't mean that God has removed them.

Consequences happen whenever we seek to act as an owner over what God has entrusted us with to steward. Again, God does not share ownership. As Romans 11:36 states, "For from Him and through Him and to Him are all things. To Him be the glory forever. Amen." It's all His.

In fact, Psalm 50:10-15 even lists things God owns. This passage falls within the context of God declaring what we are to give to Him. After all, what do you give to someone who already has it all? God lets us know in these verses,

> For every beast of the forest is Mine, the cattle on a thousand hills. I know every bird of the mountains, and everything that moves in the field is Mine. If I were hungry I would not tell you, for the world is Mine, and all it contains. Shall I eat the flesh of bulls or drink the blood of male goats? Offer to God a sacrifice of thanksgiving and pay your vows to the Most High; call upon Me in the day of trouble; I shall rescue you, and you will honor Me.

Honor. We are to give God honor. That's what living as a faithful kingdom steward does—it honors God. We cannot give God anything that He doesn't already own. Which is why our thanksgiving and our vows (the things we pledge to do on behalf of His glory and advancing His kingdom) mean so much to Him. How we steward what has been given to us makes all the difference in the world. When we do that well, He says we can call upon Him and He will rescue us.

A Story of Three Stewards

In order to help us understand how kingdom stewardship works, Jesus told a parable that was recorded for us in Matthew 25. This may be a parable you are familiar with or have previously read. Even if that is true, I don't want you to skip over it. Each time you read the Scripture, God can illuminate something new to you. Take a moment to read through the entire parable again and ask Him to give you spiritual insight about your own stewardship. Matthew 25:14-30 (ESV) says,

For it will be like a man going on a journey, who called his servants and entrusted to them his property. To one he gave five talents, to another two, to another one, to each according to his ability. Then he went away. He who had received the five talents went at once and traded with them, and he made five talents more. So also he who had the two talents made two talents more. But he who had received the one talent went and dug in the ground and hid his master's money.

Now after a long time the master of those servants came and settled accounts with them. And he who had received the five talents came forward, bringing five talents more, saying, "Master, you delivered to me five talents; here, I have made five talents more." His master said to him, "Well done, good and faithful servant. You have been faithful over a little; I will set you over much. Enter into the joy of your master."

And he also who had the two talents came forward, saying, "Master, you delivered to me two talents; here, I have made two talents more." His master said to him, "Well done, good and faithful servant. You have been faithful over a little; I will set you over much. Enter into the joy of your master."

He also who had received the one talent came forward, saying, "Master, I knew you to be a hard man, reaping where you did not sow, and gathering where you scattered no seed, so I was afraid, and I went and hid your talent in the ground. Here, you have what is yours."

But his master answered him, "You wicked and slothful servant! You knew that I reap where I have not sown and gather where I scattered no seed? Then you ought to have invested my money with the bankers, and at my coming I should have received what was my own with interest. So take the talent from him and give it to him who has the ten talents. For to everyone who has will more be given, and he will have an abundance. But from the one who has not, even what he has will be taken away. And cast the worthless servant into the outer darkness. In that place there will be weeping and gnashing of teeth."

Jesus shares some straightforward and piercing principles in this parable of the stewards. A parable is simply a story from the physical world designed to teach a spiritual lesson. In this particular story, Jesus helps us understand His ownership, our stewardship, and why approaching both realities authentically matters greatly. At the start of the parable, the main character decides to go on a long journey. Prior to leaving, though, he calls three of his servants (in today's nomenclature we might call them his direct reports) and he gives each of them a different amount to steward. To one of his direct reports he gives five talents. To another he gives two talents. And to the third he gives one talent.

In the time of the telling of this parable, a "talent" was a weight of worth. It weighed roughly seventy-five pounds and would be the equivalent of about $1,400,000 today. Thus, the person who was given one talent wasn't given a small amount to manage. Each person received a significant amount of financial responsibility when they were given their talents. I'll go into this in greater detail during a later chapter, but let me set the stage briefly as we begin.

In the midst of His absence, though, we have work to do.

Each of us has been given talents by God as well. Now, I'm not talking about singing voices or sports skills, although those are considered to be talents. In the spiritual sense of the term, a talent stretches beyond mere giftings to also include the time we have been given, our abilities, and also the resources each of us has. Simply put, your time, talents, and treasures comprise the list of things you are to steward personally, in addition to relationship roles in the family, the church, and broader society.

God created the world, and He owns all that is in it. The issue that stands before us, then, is how as His managers we handle that which does not belong to us. Jesus' parable answers that question for us clearly. Casting Himself as the owner who went away for a long period of time, Jesus told a story about Himself. After all, He died on the cross, rose from the dead, and forty days later ascended into heaven. So He is now physically absent from our lives, as the owner in the parable was. In the midst of His absence, though, we have work to do.

Just as the three servants had been entrusted with possessions that were not theirs, we have also been entrusted with that which is not ours. Their story is our story. It's up to you which character you choose to be. The first person had five talents and used his skills and resources to double it. By the time the master returned, he had ten talents. The second person in the story had two talents. This person also went and doubled what was given, coming up with four talents by the time the master had returned.

Jesus will not be pleased with us if we remain stagnant in the areas He's asked us to be productive in for His kingdom.

Yet the third person in the story simply dug a hole and put his talent in the ground. When the master came back, this man only had the same amount given to him at the start. Granted, he didn't lose it. But that's not the point. Status quo is not good enough when the job is to create growth. The master was not pleased with the man who did not increase that which had been given to him. In the same way, Jesus will not be pleased with us if we remain stagnant in the areas He's asked us to be productive in for His kingdom.

A Time of Accounting

Many of us have been given many years to advance God's kingdom agenda with the time, talents, and treasures placed in our care. God has given each of us time. He's given us abilities. He's given us resources. When we stand before Jesus on the day of judgment, He will look at how much better off His kingdom is because of how we handled what He gave us.

You see, Jesus is coming back. It may not always feel like it when you get caught up in the busy speed of life. But He will return. And when He does return, there will be an accounting. He will hold an audit. In this audit, questions will be asked about how you and I advanced His name, His kingdom, and His possessions on earth. All that we have has been given to us temporarily to work with until He returns. Second Corinthians 5:10 tells us we will give an account. It says, "For we must all appear before the judgment seat of Christ, so that each of us may receive what is due us for the things done while in the body, whether good or bad" (NIV).

We also read in 1 Corinthians 3:12-15 that the value and authenticity of what we do will be divinely evaluated:

> If anyone builds on this foundation using gold, silver, costly stones, wood, hay or straw, their work will be shown for what it is, because the Day will bring it to light. It will be revealed with fire, and the fire will test the quality of each person's work. If what has been built survives, the builder will receive a reward. If it is burned up, the builder will suffer loss but yet will be saved— even though only as one escaping through the flames. (NIV)

When you or I stand before Jesus at the judgment seat of Christ, He is going to ask us to give an account. We will have to tell Him how we used our time, talents, and treasures for Him. We won't be able to fudge the lines or exaggerate what we did because He already knows. He's already seen it. There will be a record of everything. We will, as it were, have been caught on tape. He will conduct a thorough audit of every thought and action. Only what was done for Him and His purposes will last.

You may be similar to the first two servants in the parable we read earlier, who doubled the talents given to them. In that case, you will hear as they did, "Well done, good and faithful servant. You have been faithful over a little; I will set you over much. Enter into the joy of your master." If that's you, then good. But if not, watch out. Because if you are similar to the third servant, who hid his talent in the ground, things don't look bright at all.

Let's take a look at the third servant's motivation. As we saw earlier in the passage, the man hid the talent in the ground out of fear. He knew that the master was a difficult man who reaped where he did not sow and gathered where he had scattered no seed. So instead of running the risk of losing anything, this man stuck his treasure in what he felt would be a safe place.

Seems reasonable enough, right? The master's reply lets us know that it is not. He didn't pat the man on the shoulder and thank him for protecting his assets. He didn't tell him that everything would be okay. No, he called him a wicked, lazy servant. The reason he was lazy was because even if he just took the effort to put the talent in a bank where it could grow interest, he would have had more to give the master when he returned. That wouldn't have been hard to do. But he didn't even do that. Granted, it might have been a low amount of interest but at least it would have been something. It would have shown some level of care. It would demonstrate some degree of initiative. But obviously this third person had neither care nor initiative. So he dug a hole and hid his talent until his master returned.

Many labels could have applied to this man but Jesus chose *slothful* (or lazy) and *wicked*. Now, don't misunderstand. Lazy doesn't mean this man merely wanted to sit around all day long. Lazy refers to that bent in a person to give priority to their own life and choices. Lazy says things like, "I'm not going out there to serve some master. I've got my own stuff to do. I've got my own priorities. I'm not going to sweat or waste my energy on someone else." This man may have been one of the busiest people in town, but he was busy doing all the wrong things.

Sound familiar?

It probably sounds familiar to far too many of us. After all, American culture is the busiest it has ever been. In fact, many now consider "being busy" one of the highest status symbols a person can have.[1] But being busy doing all the wrong things won't cut it.

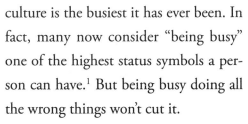

Many now consider "being busy" one of the highest status symbols a person can have. But being busy doing all the wrong things won't cut it.

Not only that, the master called this man "wicked." His motives spoke from the hole in the ground. If he had put the money in a bank, that bank would have kept a record of the deposit. But when you put money in a hole you dig in the ground, there is no record. Only you know where it is and who it really belongs to. It's like putting money under your mattress. Only you know that the money is under your mattress. Thus, he wanted to keep his evil intentions secret.

This man chose to bury the money in order to play the end against the middle. Because if the master returns, he has his money to give back to him. But if his master doesn't return, he gets to keep the money and no one knows any differently. He set himself up to steal the money if the opportunity arose, which is exactly why the master called him wicked. This servant knew the master had high expectations. He knew he was a hard man with large demands. He knew he didn't accept cheap leftovers. But his theology (what he knew) never affected his "footology" (what he did). His theology never influenced his lifestyle. It never impacted how he chose to spend his time, talents, and treasures. It's the same for far too many in church today.

Coming to church is not to be the sum total of your investment in advancing the kingdom of God. You can't stand before the judgment seat of Christ and say, "At least I came to church. At least I did the minimum requirement. At least I said 'You are good all the time and all the time, You are good.' At least I sang." No, spending your life on *your* purposes, priorities, pleasures, and *your* search for greater personal power is both lazy and wicked in the kingdom economy. Those are harsh terms, but it's not my parable. It's Jesus' parable, and those are the words He chose.

> *Coming to church is not to be the sum total of your investment in advancing the kingdom of God.*

The man dug the hole because he didn't take his master's return seriously. He had his doubts. He knew his master could get sick, be harmed, or change his plans. So he hid his talent for himself. Now, Jesus can't get sick, be harmed, or change His plans but far too many believers today doubt His return. They ask questions in their faith, at least inwardly if not outwardly, such as:

Is this real?
Have I been believing a dream?
Is faith a lie?
Is the Resurrection a lie?
Do heaven and hell truly exist?

While most who have these questions don't go around talking about these doubts openly, the fact that they have these doubts shows up in their feet. Because if you really believe that Jesus is coming back and you will have to give an account for your time, talents, and treasures—it will impact your feet. It will impact your words. It will impact your choices, investments, prayers, service, and even the depth of your love toward others and toward God.

But if you don't believe that He's coming back and that there really is going to be an accounting for what you did on earth, then you wind up being satisfied with just a little bit of religion. Just enough to be considered safe. You play the ends against the middle with a little bit of church, a little bit of the Bible, a little bit of Christianity with some Jesus sprinkled on top.

Friend, what you believe impacts what you do.

What you believe also impacts your future, just as it impacted the future of the lazy and wicked servant. As we saw in the parable, the master's response to him left little room for confusion. Let's review Matthew 25:28-30,

> So take the talent from him and give it to him who has the ten talents. For to everyone who has will more be given, and he will have an abundance. But from the one who has not, even what he has will be taken away. And cast the worthless servant into the outer darkness. In that place there will be weeping and gnashing of teeth. (NIV)

Jesus made it clear that the stuff the man hid in hopes of gaining from it would be immediately taken from him and given to the one who had the ten talents. It was given to the man who maximized his kingdom potential. Jesus tells us that God is willing to take back what He has given to someone if He does not feel that person is putting it to good use. It's His possession so He has the right to do that. He can take opportunities or time, talents, and treasures back and give them to the person who has demonstrated faithful kingdom-use of what they already had.

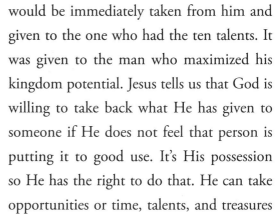

Friend, what you believe impacts what you do.

More than that, though, Jesus tells us through this story that the man was then thrown out to a place of great mourning and sadness. It's easy to think this place is hell but it is not. The master in this story owns these servants. They are his, and the issue at hand was reward for their work—not their eternal salvation. Spiritually speaking, that means once you are a child of Jesus, you do not run the risk of losing your salvation. A person is not saved based on works (Romans 4:4-5; Ephesians 2:8-9). You are saved by grace through faith alone in Christ alone for the forgiveness of sins, and are given the gift of eternal life. Once converted, however, you are saved for work (Ephesians 2:10). These works position you for usefulness and rewards in God's heavenly kingdom.

When looking back over their lives and how they spent them, there will be many things people will wish they could change.

The terms "outer darkness" and "weeping and gnashing of teeth" are not referring to hell. Rather, these are Semitic phrases that mean "profound regret." Regret will be a reality at the judgment seat of Christ (1 Corinthians 3:10-15; 1 John 2:28). In fact, many Christians will face varying levels of regret. When looking back over their lives and how they spent them, there will be many things people will wish they could change.

The Millennial Kingdom

When Jesus returns, He is returning to establish His millennial kingdom. This is where Jesus will reign for one thousand years. When Christ comes, He will make His entrance on the Mount of Olives just outside the old city of Jerusalem. He will come through what is now a boarded-up gate called the Eastern Gate and to set up His throne in order to rule the earth with a rod of iron. He will rule by force. There will be no rebellion under Jesus' one-thousand-year rule. None. The earth will exist during that period of time exactly as God intended it to be. The wolf will lie down with the lamb. Heaven's influence and manifestation will be experienced on earth entirely (Isaiah 11:1-9).

During this time, Jesus will assign believers to varying levels of responsibility based on their faithfulness as kingdom stewards. Some will get to rule over cities. Some will be positioned over states. Some will govern communities. There will be a variety of roles determined by the level of service to the King in the previous age.

Now, not everyone is going to be as excited about their respective assignments and roles. Some people will experience great regret because they will be in a position of less influence than they had during their life on earth. They will be able to look around them and see what other people are doing but will be assigned to serve in the position they have earned.

When I was a teenager, one of the things my dad would do when he could afford it was to take us to an amusement park in Baltimore. It was called Gwynn Oak Amusement Park. I absolutely loved that place. I loved the rides, roller coasters, and food. In fact, the wilder the ride, the more exciting it was for me. I'll never forget my three siblings piling into the car with me and heading to the amusement park with my dad.

Yet on one particular occasion, I had been misbehaving. So my father used this as an opportunity to teach me a lesson. He told all of us to hop in the car to head to the amusement park, but when he got there he did something that has stuck with me all of these years. First, he handed equal amounts of tickets out to each of us. Then, he reached over to my tickets and took them back. He went on to hand out my tickets to my sister and two brothers. As I'm standing there in disbelief over what is happening right before my eyes, my dad turns to me and says, "Tony, you have not been behaving yourself so you don't get to ride today."

Once he said that, there was weeping and gnashing of teeth! My dad took me to the park so I could see the rides. He took me into the proximity of smelling the food. Then he made me sit there and watch everyone else enjoy themselves. You can be assured that I learned my lesson.

Similarly, every believer in Jesus will enter heaven. But not every believer will get tickets. Not every believer will be entrusted with roles and responsibilities that will excite them. See, heaven is free. The price has already been paid. But the rewards in heaven are determined by what you do as a kingdom steward while on earth.

Friend, if all you see is what is in front of you right now and you don't authentically believe that Jesus is coming back and that His rewards are going to blow your mind, then you are going to function as an owner on earth rather than a manager. You are going to waste your time, talents, and treasures rather than invest them. The mindset of a kingdom steward, then, is that of an investor and not a spender. Investors ask and answer two strategic questions: *What will be the long-term generational kingdom impact of my life in history?* and *What difference will that impact make for eternity?*

But if you are willing to take the faith-risk in believing that everything belongs to God and that He wants you to use it for His glory in advancing His kingdom, you will experience an incredible reality when you enter heaven. If you will adopt and apply the worldview of a kingdom steward, based on God's Word, I can guarantee you that He will blow your mind when He calls you for your audit. Now, you can't change yesterday. Yesterday is done. You may have squandered what God gave you. But you can do a lot about today, and even more about tomorrow.

Remember, this life is merely a warm-up and dress rehearsal for the life that is to come.

3

MOTIVATION

When my kids were young and still living at home, I would always bring them back a gift when I traveled. If preaching or an event took me on the road, I would try not to come home empty-handed. Whether it was something small I picked up at the airport or something I was able to take time to stop and get, I did my best to make it memorable.

As I came through the door each time after a trip, all four kids would grab me and hug me and I would hug them back. I was immediately surrounded by love and the words, "Daddy's home! Daddy's home!" After a moment or two of this, I would reach in my bag or briefcase and pull out their surprises. Squeals of delight echoed in the entryway, then quick scurrying as each kid darted away to their respective locations to look at their gift.

In time, I would get the question, "When are you leaving again?" No joke. My kids actually wanted me to leave more because after the gift-giving routine had gone on long enough, they got so used to receiving what I brought them that they wanted more. In fact, eventually the hugs got a bit shorter, the shrieks got a little quieter, and the hands went out for the gifts a lot faster. They got so used to the blessings I would bring that they could skip me altogether to get to the goodies.

What happened to my kids often happens with God's kids. They get so used to His goodness and favor that they don't mind Him not being there as long as He continues to bring the gifts.

We're living in a day when people want God's blessings without God.

They want the benefits without the Being.

They want the rewards without the Relationship.

But that's all mixed up. That's backwards. That's similar to an extraordinary exchange in Scripture between God and Moses. Essentially, God told Moses that he was to take the Israelites into the Promised Land. He promised to send an angel before them in order to pave the way. He guaranteed the defeat of their enemies while simultaneously describing for Moses a land flowing with milk and honey. Bottom line: God told Moses that he and his people would receive guidance, protection, provision, and blessing.

But there is one thing God would not give them, due to their own obstinate ways: Himself. We read, "Go up to a land flowing with milk and honey; for I will not go up in your midst, because you are an obstinate people, and I might destroy you on the way" (Exodus 33:3).

The Israelites had been greenlit to go, with one caveat. They would go without God.

But Moses knew better than that.

Moses knew that the blessings of God were no match for the presence of God. He knew that milk and honey by the barrel meant nothing without the Source of that provision. Moses was wise enough to decline the offered blessings and push back with his own request,

> Now therefore, I pray You, if I have found favor in Your sight,
> let me know Your ways that I may know You, so that I may find
> favor in Your sight. Consider too, that this nation is Your people.
> EXODUS 33:13

God heard Moses' heart. He saw his motivation. Moses didn't strive for significance, success, or his own personal platform. If he did, this would have been his chance. Get God off to the sidelines, stick an angel in front, and push forward. Claim the land. Destroy the enemies. Drink the milk. Bathe in the honey. Go down in history as the greatest leader the Israelites—no, the world—had ever had.

But as I said earlier, Moses knew better than that. In fact, knowing better than that is why Moses was such a great leader after all. Moses had enough discernment to know that to go anywhere without God was foolishness. So, he didn't go on his own. More than that, he appealed to God's heart in his response, "Let me know Your ways that I may know You."

Moses had enough discernment to know that to go anywhere without God was foolishness.

In other words, Moses made it clear that this wasn't just about knowing the strategies to build his nation's brand or establish his people as a dominant force. No, he let God know that the blessings without the Blesser were no blessings at all. This was all about God: Loving Him. Knowing Him. Worshiping Him. Honoring Him. Experiencing Him. Journeying with Him. Understanding Him.

To say that the heart of God melted might be a bit of an anthropomorphic stretch, but His response indicates it just might have. God replied, possibly with a half-smile and a sigh, "My presence shall go with you, and I will give you rest" (Exodus 33:14). Not only did God promise His presence, He also promised them the ability to enjoy the blessings He had previously agreed to give plus more. He promised the provision of rest.

So many people today have successfully accumulated this, that, and the other, but they have done so at the expense of the ability to actually enjoy it all. Being busy is the new American idol. It's almost considered a bragging right to answer someone who is asking, "How you are doing?"

with the phrase, "I'm just so busy, but otherwise I'm fine." To constantly be on the go is the contemporary status symbol for success.

But that's not how it is in biblical blessings. We have been sold a lie from Satan that we bought cheaply because it's a lie that appeals to our own egos. But Proverbs 10:22 tells us, "It is the blessing of the LORD that makes rich, and He adds no sorrow to it."

We often think of "sorrow" as pain, tears, or loss. But sorrow can come clothed in a variety of outfits. These include restlessness, a lack of contentment, unease, and a persistent drive for the next best and biggest thing. But God's blessings, when they are truly His blessings, come with none of that. They come with rest.

Moses knew that. Which is exactly why Moses quickly declined God's offer of provisions without His presence. Perhaps he had climbed that ladder before in Pharaoh's house and knew that power and prestige come coupled with emptiness and worry. Moses didn't want the blessings. He didn't want the gifts. He wanted God. So much so that after God said He would go with them, Moses pushed his request a bit further. He had gotten what he wanted. God had agreed to go. But Moses wanted more. He cried out in Exodus 33:18, "Show me Your glory!" Moses wanted to see God.

Knowing that Moses could not see Him and live, God then gently tucked him away in the cleft of a rock and covered him with His hand as He passed by, allowing Moses to get a glimpse of what no human had seen outside of the perfect garden, and lived to tell: God's manifested glory. In first declining the blessings, Moses got to see a greater blessing—the beauty of the glory of God.

We're living in a day when all of that has been flipped and people seem to want God only for what they can get from Him. They don't just want Him because of who He is and what He has already done. The motivation has shifted from desiring to see *His* glory to desiring to see their own. But having a biblical motivation for kingdom stewardship is key to carrying out your divine destiny to its fullest. You might be surprised that I've chosen to start out this book on stewardship by focusing on knowing God. Most discussions on the topic of stewardship center on money tips and financial advice. Yes, kingdom stewardship does involve how you handle your money, but as you will come to see, it involves so much more. And until you operate according to the biblical concept of stewardship, you will not be experiencing the benefits of a good and faithful steward. In essence, you will have chosen to go into the Promised Land without God rather than focusing on God as Moses did. This is where stewardship should focus—on God alone.

A Response to God's Grace

So, let's start with our mindset. A correct mindset makes all the difference in the world. In 2 Corinthians 9:8 we discover the root of this biblical motivation for kingdom stewardship. The root rests in God's grace. We read, "And God is able to make all grace abound to you, so that always having all sufficiency in everything, you may have an abundance for every good deed." Read that verse again. It's one of my favorites because that verse contains all you need to know to fully live out God's calling on your life and to experience His goodness. Friend, God does not want you to be manipulated into serving Him or to be motivated by selfish gain.

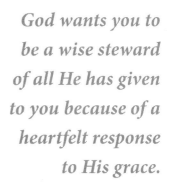

God wants you to be a wise steward of all He has given to you because of a heartfelt response to His grace.

God wants you to be a wise steward of all He has given to you because of a heartfelt response to His grace.

Grace can be defined as God's inexhaustible supply of goodness that He does for you. It involves those things you cannot do for yourself. Grace comes to you as unmerited favor. It's something you can never earn, would never be able to repay, and can never run out of.

All of life is the result of God's grace. So awesome is grace that Paul calls it God's indescribable gift (2 Corinthians 9:14-15).

Keep in mind, grace is always free. Scripture tells us in Romans 11:6 that grace is given apart from works. As soon as someone seeks to deserve grace, they have nullified and canceled it right then and there. We read, "But if it is by grace, it is no longer on the basis of works, otherwise grace is no longer grace."

You can't get it through anything you do. You can't even buy it. In Acts 8 we read the story of a man named Simon who had wowed the crowds and created a large following through his ability to practice magic and perform signs. When Simon saw the crowds who followed the disciples as they preached about Jesus, as well as the accompanying signs and wonders the disciples performed, he asked if he could buy that same power himself. We read, "Now when Simon saw that the Spirit was bestowed through the laying on of the apostles' hands, he offered them money" (Acts 8:18).

Peter rebuked him harshly when he said,

> May your silver perish with you, because you thought you could obtain the gift of God with money! You have no part or portion in this matter, for your heart is not right before God. Therefore repent of this wickedness of yours, and pray the Lord that, if possible, the intention of your heart may be forgiven you.
> ACTS 8:20-22

God's grace isn't for sale. His presence isn't a prize you win for good works. His power comes to hearts who authentically seek to know Him and steward what has been given to them out of a spirit of gratitude and love.

Far too many Christians today are seeking to manipulate God. That may sound harsh, but it's true. Sure, they may be able to manipulate others and even create for themselves a large following, but no one manipulates God. No one. God sees the heart and gives grace to those who know they do not deserve it and could not live without it. Those are the hearts that respond with worship.

Ephesians 2:7 gives us a glimpse into the preeminent role grace plays not only now but for all eternity. It says, "So that in the ages to come He might show the surpassing riches of His grace in kindness toward us in Christ Jesus." Grace is never-ending. There will be so much grace in heaven that it will blow your mind. In fact, God will even remove night and our desire for sleep so that we can stay awake all the time in order to fully bask in the glory of His grace (Revelation 22:5). That's how much this supernatural provision of grace in eternity will be.

> *Everything God is going to do for you, He has already done. Your part is not to cajole God into doing more; your part is to access what He has already done.*

But that's for later. What about the here and now? While you and I cannot earn grace, manipulate God for it, or even pay enough money to get it, we can discover spiritual principles on how to access it. Accessing grace doesn't create more grace, it allows us to tap into all that God has established for us to have. As a kingdom steward, the ability to access grace which serves as the funnel for all you have is critical in living your life to the maximum experience and impact. Ephesians 1:3 says that God has already blessed us. We read, "Blessed be the God and Father of our Lord Jesus Christ, who has blessed us with every spiritual blessing in the heavenly places in Christ." Everything God is going to do for you, He has already done. Your part is not to cajole God into doing more; your part is to access what He has already done.

So how do you access His grace? Through faith. Romans 5:1-2 states it this way:

> Therefore, having been justified by faith, we have peace with
> God through our Lord Jesus Christ, through whom also we have
> obtained our introduction by faith into this grace in which we
> stand; and we exult in hope of the glory of God.

God's unmerited favor for believers has already been deposited into your life's account. But it is up to you to access it. A few years ago, I gave each of our executive staff at the church an iPad for Christmas. The iPad came fully loaded with everything an iPad contains. Each had an equal amount of benefits they could gain from using the iPad. But each did not access the iPad at the same level. Some used it all the time. Others used it part of the time. And then some stuck it in a drawer and didn't use it at all. Similarly, God has given us all of His spiritual blessings and favor. Through Jesus Christ, we have been given access to the full power of His glory, which provides us the ability to steward the full realization of His will for our lives. Some believers access this grace fully. Yet others access it partially. And still others stick it away, only to be forgotten.

My mom was a Scrabble Queen in her day. She could beat anyone and everyone at that game. I never could figure out how she could use the same set of twenty-six letters I was using and come up with so many words. She just knew how to do it. She knew how to arrange them, connect them, and play them in her favor. Now, when a Scrabble player is looking to come up with additional words, they don't go and create new letters. All of the letters already exist. Scrabble is simply about the access and arrangement of those letters in order to make as many high-scoring words as possible.

Likewise, God has given us His grace, and that grace is comprehensive. As believers, we are not tasked with going out to look for more grace. We merely need to work with and tap into what He has already provided. In order to do so, you will need to approach your time, talents, and treasures with what I call a "grace mindset." It's a grace orientation that sets you up to tap into the treasures of His unending favor. Moses modeled this mindset for us when he resisted God's offer of provision, protection, and blessing apart from His presence. Moses knew that none of that meant anything if it came without an ongoing relationship to God Himself.

In the church age, you and I are to look to Jesus Christ, who is the dispenser of the grace and goodness we so desperately need.

As a kingdom steward, when you learn to view all of life through the lens of grace, you will discover what God gave to Moses as a result of his request. You will learn the power, blessing, and spiritual productivity located in God's gift of rest. Moses had to look to God to gain entry into the glory of His grace. In the church age, you and I are to look to Jesus Christ, who is the dispenser of the grace and goodness we so desperately need. Let's examine a few verses that paint this picture for us:

> And the Word became flesh, and dwelt among us, and we saw His glory, glory as of the only begotten from the Father, full of grace and truth.
> JOHN 1:14

> For of His fullness we have all received, and grace upon grace.
> JOHN 1:16

> For the grace of God has appeared, bringing salvation to all men.
> TITUS 2:11

Grace, then, is more than a theological doctrine. It is a Person. In Jesus is found this "grace upon grace." The picture of these words is like water flowing in on a shore where one wave comes after another wave, and it never stops. Christian author Max Lucado recently shared how he was sitting on the seashore in Hawaii with his granddaughter watching the waves roll in, when she asked him when it would be turned off. He smiled and replied, "It keeps going. This doesn't get turned off."[1] Neither does God's grace. Wave upon wave of His grace has been given to each of us through the life of His Son Jesus Christ. You can't use it up. You can't exhaust it. You can't lose it. It's always there. Always free. Always available. But you do have to access it through faith. You have to know it's there and believe it's yours to receive it.

It's like the man who went on a cruise and when he walked off the boat on the last day, one of the crew asked him how his trip was. The man told him that the ship was nice but he had a miserable time. When the crew member inquired why, the man explained that he was starving. The ticket to the trip had cost so much that he didn't have money left over for food.

What this man failed to understand, believe, and apply was that the entirety of the food on the ship had already been included in the price of the ticket. The food was free. All he needed to do was access it.

Built Into the Seed

If you really want to understand how grace operates in relationship to stewarding your life's resources, you must think agriculturally. You must think like a farmer. Second Corinthians 9:6-10 sets this up for us:

> Now this I say, he who sows sparingly will also reap sparingly, and he who sows bountifully will also reap bountifully. Each one must do just as he has purposed in his heart, not grudgingly or under compulsion, for God loves a cheerful giver. And God is able to make all grace abound to you, so that always having all

sufficiency in everything, you may have an abundance for every good deed; as it is written,

"He scattered abroad, he gave to the poor,
His righteousness endures forever."

Now He who supplies seed to the sower and bread for food will supply and multiply your seed for sowing and increase the harvest of your righteousness.

Within this passage lies the quintessential understanding of how to access grace. Grace is built into the seed itself. Consider a farmer with a crop of corn. When the farmer plants a seed of corn, a stalk forms and grows to bear ears of corn itself later on. All of this came from the seed. Now, in the new corn that has grown are new seeds for more corn. In this way, using the seed enables the farmer to gain access to even more seeds.

Even though everything comes from God, the farmer still has a part to play. You will never find a farmer reaping a crop he did not sow.

The way this translates into our understanding of accessing God's grace is that God has placed within grace the seed of grace itself. It's built in. So, since grace is built into the seed, the way you gain access to greater grace is through the sowing (planting) of a seed of grace.

Now, there is a process to sowing a seed. To sow, a farmer tills the soil and drops the seed in the ground. When he drops the seed in the ground, he has now become totally dependent on God. The soil and its nutrients come from God. The rain sent to water it comes from God. The sunshine that brings it energy for growth comes from God. The DNA within the seed itself comes from God. Everything that is responsible for this little seed to become all it was created to be is sourced in God. In fact, God even supplied the seed to begin with (2 Corinthians 9:10).

Yet even though everything comes from God, the farmer still has a part to play. You will never find a farmer reaping a crop he did not sow. You will never overhear him saying that he is waiting for a crop to produce that which he did not plant. You will never see him standing by the empty field convinced that stuff will grow even though he put no seeds in the ground.

No, the farmer has an active part to play. He has to plant the seeds.

The process of the seed's development belongs to God. But the sowing of the seed belongs to the farmer.

What if Farmer Brown decided that rather than planting seeds this year, he would just pray and believe that he had a crop? Even if he persisted in elaborate prayers indicating his full trust in God to provide his crop, there would be no crop. Yes, even if Farmer Brown fasted and prayed, there would be no crop. Farmer Brown's responsibility was to sow the seed. If he skipped that, then he couldn't expect to reap a crop. Any farmer knows that.

But it seems that many Christians do not.

Similar to farming, God has revealed an invaluable principle which ushers in benefits into your life of stewardship. Sowing produces reaping, through this manner:

God supplies the seed.
You sow the seed.
God causes the growth.
You reap.

It's pretty simple and straightforward and yet so many believers look to complicate it somehow. One of the ways we complicate it is through our pride. This isn't new to our culture today. This showed up in biblical culture as well. We read about this in Paul's letter to the Corinthian church where he writes in response to followers seeking to link up with a brand, name, or platform other than Jesus Christ,

> What then is Apollos? And what is Paul? Servants through whom you believed, even as the Lord gave opportunity to each one. I planted, Apollos watered, but God was causing the growth. So then neither the one who plants nor the one who waters is anything, but God who causes the growth. Now he who plants and he who waters are one; but each will receive his own reward according to his own labor. For we are God's fellow workers; you are God's field, God's building.
>
> I CORINTHIANS 3:5-9

God provides both the seed and all that is necessary for the growth of that seed. Understanding that is crucial to stewarding life with a grace mindset. Yet even though grace is embedded in the seed itself, you and I do need to sow it. No bank pays you interest when no deposits are made.

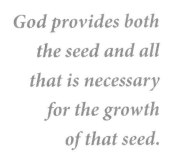

God provides both the seed and all that is necessary for the growth of that seed.

In Luke 6:38, God outlines for us a process that He established as a way of accessing His provision in the seed. It reads, "Give, and it will be given to you. They will pour into your lap a good measure—pressed down, shaken together, and running over. For by your standard of measure it will be measured to you in return." From this verse, I have termed what I call the "Theology of It." The "Theology of It" is based on a principle that God established at creation.

When you plant a pear seed, you get a pear tree. When you plant an apple seed, you get an apple tree. You will never plant a watermelon seed and grow a squash. This is true simply because God established replication to occur after each seed's own kind. Whatever it is that you plant is what you will get back.

Faith and Actions

What serves as a principle for creation is broadened into a principle for life in Luke 6:38. Jesus said, "Give, and it will be given to you." By this principle, the thing you give is also the thing you will receive. This is critical to understanding how to fully live as a kingdom steward. If you have a need, make sure you sow a seed in the life of someone else in the same area as your own personal need. Don't just ask God to meet your need without making sure you plant the seed. God longs to meet your many needs and in Luke 6:38, He has given you the wisdom on how this can be done.

Luke 6:38 places before us an exciting and rewarding opportunity. Based on this principle, you can get very specific with God. If you are facing a financial need, look around you and see how you can help someone else financially, even if it's with a minimal amount. Do you have an emotional need for comfort? Then see how you can comfort someone else. In this passage we discover a powerful tool for accessing the graces of God on a greater, more tangible level. This is when your need is actually in the seed.

A widow in Zarephath was down to her last meal (1 Kings 17). She lived in a day and location of uncertainty. There were no government handouts. There was probably very little by way of charity. All she had to feed herself and her son was a little bit of flour and an even smaller amount of oil. Even so, this is who God instructed to feed the prophet Elijah.

Elijah came to the widow and asked her to make a bread cake for him, as well as to give him some water. In an act of extreme faith, even though she was afraid, she did just that. She gave Elijah the thing that her son and she needed the most: food. In return, Elijah told her that her jar of flour would not run out and her oil would not cease until rain returned to the land.

The widow got back the very thing she had given away: food. Just as God had promised, her jar of flour and her oil did not run out, giving her household plenty to eat until the rains returned to water the earth. It took faith for this widow to give away her last bit of food, just as it takes faith for you to give something you need to someone else. But remember, faith is much more than words. Faith always involves actions; it involves your feet. That's why we have been instructed to *walk* by faith, not just to *talk* by faith.

> *Faith always involves actions; it involves your feet. That's why we have been instructed to walk by faith, not just to talk by faith.*

Hannah was a woman who couldn't get pregnant (1 Samuel 1). For years she tried, but was never able. In biblical culture, barrenness was akin to a curse in many ways. As a result, Hannah was often depressed because of her situation. She was also mocked by others. One year when Hannah went to the temple, she employed the "Theology of It." She said, "God, if You'll give me a son, I'll give him back to You." Which is exactly what she did when God gave her a son the very next year.

But the story doesn't end there. If you read on, you'll discover that after Hannah gave her son to God, God gave Hannah a "pressed down, shaken together, and running over" return on her investment of giving her son to the Lord. Hannah's empty quiver became full when she gave back to God (and subsequently the people of Israel) the very thing she needed and had asked for. As a result, she had five more children.

Give, and it will be given to you.

We see a similar situation in the New Testament when we come across over five thousand men, not including women and children, who had been following Jesus for several days and were hungry (John 6). As the people began to complain of hunger and the disciples began to fret about what to do, Jesus asked the disciples how they were going to feed so many. They needed something to eat, so He asked the disciples to find some food.

All the disciples could find was a young boy with some sardines and crackers. The little boy's lunch was exactly what they needed but it was also the little boy's lunch. We often overlook the fact that this little boy was no doubt hungry himself. For him to give up his lunch was no small sacrifice. And yet he gave to Jesus the very thing that everyone, including himself, needed—food.

When the gift of food—"it"—was given to Jesus, Jesus blessed it, thanked God, and turned "it" into enough food to feed everyone with plenty left over. All Christ started with was a seed planted, a bag of food. But when that seed was offered and blessed, it became an overabundance of food to those in need. The boy received back more than he gave up.

When God sees faith through our actions and not just our words, He responds.

The widow of Zarephath, Hannah, and this young boy were all living out what it means to be a horizontal Jesus to those around them. They were willing to give from their want and lack so that others could gain, and to do so in the name of God, as a result of their faith in God. Because they lived as a horizontal Jesus to one another, a miracle showed up in their vertical relationship with God.

The problem today is people want God to manufacture a miracle when they're unwilling to give what they have to anyone else around them, which usually means they're not exercising any faith at all, or their motivation has no connection to the glory of God and the advancement of His kingdom. But when God sees faith through our actions and not just our words, He responds.

So if you want to be forgiven, for example, then give forgiveness. If you need love, give love. If you are seeking a promotion on your job, then give extra at the office or seek to assist or employ someone else, whether that be a neighbor's kid to mow your lawn or something else. If you want to grow your business, then help someone else grow theirs. If you want to grow spiritually, invest in the spiritual growth of others. Whatever it is, give the "it" that you want to be returned to you. The solution to your need is in the thing you sow when it's connected to God as the source. This is how God's principle of "reverse reciprocity" works.

The biblical story of Ruth shows us how Ruth gave her aging mother-in-law the security of a relationship with her, and as a result Ruth received the security of a relationship with a husband later on. Another example is Job, who lost everything. He lost his finances, home, and family. Yet when he prayed for the well-being of his friends and asked God to show them kindness, God turned Job's situation around and showered him with abundance and provisions as well. More than he had even lost.

God's Abundant Giving

Let's look at Luke 6:38 a bit more deeply before closing this chapter. Jesus said "they" will pour out a blessing to you. Who are "they"? "They" are whomever God chooses to use to meet your need. God has a supply of need-meeters that He can call upon as seed planters. Jesus continued, "They will pour into your lap a good measure—pressed down, shaken together, and running over." To understand what Jesus is saying, you need to think agriculturally. Jesus was speaking about grain.

In New Testament days, a person would go to a merchant and ask for a certain measure of wheat. The merchant would scoop out the measure the person ordered, whatever size it was, but the merchant would only put in about three-fourths of the full measure. Then he would shake the person's sack or container to fill in the gaps before adding the rest of the grain so the buyer would get his full order without any gaps, which might make the container appear to be full when it wasn't. But that's not all. The merchant would then press down on the grain to create room for more.

Jesus used this common practice to illustrate the abundance of God's giving—and He took it another step by saying that when God pours into your sack, He does so until the blessing is "running over."

God says when you give "it" to someone else, He then uses "they" to meet your need based on the "it" that you gave. And when He does it, He does it in such a way that He creates room for more. This excites me because it is spiritually based; that is, it's not just wanting things for our own sake. This principle also helps to explain why so many of us believers are not seeing more of God show up on every level in our lives. We are not seeing God show up in our experience of our relationship with Him because we are refusing to give "it" in our relationships with others. The problem is that we want to get our needs met from God without being willing to give to anyone else.

> *Being a conduit for blessing is critical to experiencing true blessing from God.*

A lot of Christians want to be blessed, but they don't want to give more of themselves—their time, talents, and treasures—to God for the benefit of others. They want their needs met in the pressed down, shaken together way Jesus described in Luke 6:38 without fulfilling the principles and precepts of the "one anothers." Being a conduit for blessing is critical to experiencing true blessing from God.

Jesus brings the point home in the last statement of this verse:

"For by your standard of measure it will be measured to you in return." If you give God only a thimble to fill, that's all you will get back in return.

This is the secret to maximizing your life as a kingdom steward. In Deuteronomy 24:19, God told the Israelites, "When you reap your harvest in your field and have forgotten a sheaf in the field, you shall not go back to get it; it shall be for the alien, for the orphan, and for the widow, in order that the LORD your God may bless you in all the work of your hands." God says when you leave part of your crop for the needy—when you plant a seed for others—He will bless you. That is just one of several clear biblical pictures of how our relationship with others can affect the expression of our relationship with God.

Remember, a blessing is not just what God does for you, but also what He knows He is free to do through you. God told Abraham, "I am going to bless you," and then He said, "And through you all the nations of the earth will be blessed" (my translation, Genesis 12:3).

This is why Jesus' words are recorded in Acts 20:35: "It is more blessed to give than to receive." The reason Jesus said that is because when God knows He can flow through you, He will flow ever more greatly to you. But the moment God sees it's only about you, that it's going to stop with you and not flow through you to someone else, He is not as interested in continuing to flow to you. He wants conduit and not cul-de-sac followers. This is one of the primary reasons you need to be intentionally plugged into a local body of believers. This is the key context, outside of your family, where you can live out your stewardship since it is God's spiritual family He wants us to minister to first (Galatians 6:10).

In the church context, and others, you are positioned to give "it" to God by giving "it" to others, and "it" will flow back to you in poured-out blessing. This is a promise not just related to money but any category of need in your life, whether encouragement, love, healing, or anything else.

The Motivation for Stewardship

Thus, the motivation for kingdom stewardship is to be grace. Free. Abundant. Provided grace. It is injected into the seed. But the seed has to be sown for a harvest to be produced. A lot of us are waiting on God when God is actually waiting on us. He wants to see something planted, not just something requested. Proverbs 11:24-28 summarizes the law of sowing and reaping this way:

> There is one who scatters, and yet increases all the more, and there is one who withholds what is justly due, and yet it results only in want. The generous man will be prosperous, and he who waters will himself be watered. He who withholds grain, the people will curse him, but blessing will be on the head of him who sells it. He who diligently seeks good seeks favor, but he who seeks evil, evil will come to him. He who trusts in his riches will fall, but the righteous will flourish like the green leaf.

This mindset is far different from that of the self-centered contemporary prosperity movement that makes getting rich an end in itself apart from the spiritual development and righteous living that God wishes to precede any focus on material gain. Spiritual development must always precede economic development (Matthew 6:33). The wisdom of Solomon puts it this way, "Cast your bread on the surface of the waters, for you will find it after many days. . . . He who watches the wind will not sow and he who looks at the clouds will not reap" (Ecclesiastes 11:1, 4). In other words, give and it will be given to you. A kingdom steward operates first and foremost from a mindset of giving because that is the mindset of grace.

Imagine with me for a moment that you are standing in a candy store with two of your kids. If you don't have kids, imagine that you do for the sake of this illustration. You are standing in one of those big candy stores with rows upon rows and bins upon bins containing all kinds of mouth-watering tasty treasures. Both of your kids want some candy but to simplify things, you fill up one large bag with some of their favorites and then hand it to your oldest. You make sure to let him know that he needs to share it with his younger sister whenever she wants any. There is one bag, but what is inside the bag is intended for them both. Your oldest is not the owner; he is the steward.

A kingdom steward operates first and foremost from a mindset of giving because that is the mindset of grace.

However, in time, you notice that your oldest child is hoarding all of the candy, only grudgingly giving a piece to his sister when she cries. What will you do? When the candy runs out, will you go back to the store and buy another bag to give to your oldest again? Or will you make other arrangements this time?

Conversely, what if your oldest child had done something different altogether. What if after you left the store, he began to share the contents of the bag not only with his little sister but also with other kids in your neighborhood when you got home? Each face lit up with joy as your oldest gladly handed out piece after piece of candy. What would you do this time when the candy bag ran out? Would you go back to the store and give it to your oldest again? Or would you even consider giving him more this time, seeing as it brought so much happiness to so many people?

Many parents would likely give more candy to the child who distributed it to others. And many parents would not trust the child who hoarded with any more, at least not anytime soon. It's not that our love for our child would have changed. But our child's experience of that love, demonstrated in this case through blessing and provision, would have been diminished as a result of his behavior.

We have a Father in heaven who has a very big family. His love for us is secure. He will always be our Dad. But our experience of His love—whether through blessing, provision, presence, or any number of things—will often depend on how we honor Him through how we treat the others He loves.

Give, and it will be given to you.

Hoard, and you may miss out on much of what God desires to give to you.

My son Jonathan played football for the NFL's San Diego Chargers. When he was with this team, my wife and I would fly out to attend the games. San Diego is a beautiful city with ideal weather year-round. We always enjoyed our stay there.

A unique statue stands in San Diego. It wasn't designed to be a unique statue. In fact, it had originally been carved similar to any of the thousands of statues of Jesus that dot the landscape of our world. There was nothing unusual about this statue until some vandals decided to make a statement and break off Christ's hands.

> *Living your life as a true kingdom steward means living your life as the hands and feet of Jesus.*

Make a statement, they did. I'm just not sure it's the statement they had intended. When the pastor of the church saw the vandalized Jesus without hands, he decided to leave it that way and erect a sign at the base that read, "I have no hands but yours."

Living your life as a true kingdom steward means living your life as the hands and feet of Jesus. This is one of God's means for accessing and experiencing more of His grace. You will unleash your fullest potential when you apply this principle to all that you do with your time, talents, and treasures in His name. God promises that if you sow in tears (when it is painful or you are fearful to do so), you will reap in joy (Psalm 126:5-6).

PART II

THE
SCOPE
OF
KINGDOM
STEWARDSHIP

4

STRUCTURE

If you are an American citizen, you are living here under a covenant. While America is not officially a kingdom, it resembles kingdom rule on a lot of levels. One of these involves the Constitution of the United States. This overarching governing document defines who we are as citizens, who we are as a nation, and what we ought to be both collectively and in relation to each other. It provides the structure within which we are to function.

The Constitution has a very specific focus, which is to provide the framework whereby the people under its rule live out their rights to life, liberty, and the pursuit of happiness as set forth in the Declaration of Independence. Through its original language, as well as in additional amendments, this document sets in place the context and boundaries within which we are to live.

The only qualification to access all the rights set out in this covenantal document is that of being a citizen. It doesn't matter whether you were born here or naturalized here. It doesn't matter what your background is, or your race, class, gender, or culture. Citizenship grants you the full rights and privileges as well as all the protections and provisions outlined in our Constitution.

Not everyone agrees on the interpretation and application of the content in the Constitution, which is why our nation finds itself in a constitutional crisis at the moment. Yet, even so, we are still under the overarching rule of the controlling document set up to govern all members of our country.

Growing up in America and attending public schools, at least when I was a student, we began each day by standing in place, putting our hands over our hearts, and saying the pledge of allegiance to the United States of America and to the Republic for which it stands. We repeated the words that we are "one nation under God, indivisible, with liberty and justice for all." As students we were asked to repeat this pledge day in and day out because it served as a perpetual reminder of our allegiance to the covenant of the kingdom in which we lived, breathed, and had our being.

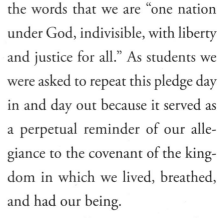

God's kingdom stewards are to pledge allegiance to the covenant that belongs to the King and thereafter seek to abide within the parameters set in place through His covenant.

As we will continue to explore throughout this book, God has a kingdom. His kingdom is controlled by a covenant. His kingdom rule rests within the established structure of this covenant. His kingdom stewards have been established by Him to manage the various aspects of the outer workings of His rule within this same structure. Thus, God's kingdom stewards are to pledge allegiance to the covenant that belongs to the King and thereafter seek to abide within the parameters set in place through His covenant.

When there are people who choose not to do so and, thus, rebel against the covenant, they have set themselves up in opposition to the King. They are no longer carrying out the role of a kingdom steward, which is to faithfully oversee the protection and expansion of the assets God has entrusted to them to manage on His behalf.

Scripture supports this role of stewardship in a myriad of places but one primary place is found in Deuteronomy 8:18, "But you shall remember the LORD your God, for it is He who is giving you power to make wealth, that He may confirm His covenant which He swore to your fathers, as it is this day." In this passage we identify the scope of a steward but we also identify the purpose God intends as an outcome for functioning within His prescribed structure. Your proper management of His resources is used by God to "confirm His covenant."

As mentioned, the covenant is God's constitution. It is to be the defining word of your spiritual existence. In the Old Testament, this covenant was tied to the law. Various rules, regulations, and laws were established for the Israelite people to follow as a reflection of their allegiance to the one true God. In the New Covenant, these laws are summed up for us in the two greatest commandments, given to us by Jesus. We are to love God and also to love others (Matthew 22:36-40). Obedience to these two commandments keeps a person aligned under the covenant.

When you discover the power of embracing God's covenant in your everyday choices and confirm its reality in what you think, say, and do, your spiritual existence will become graphically transformed because you are now functioning under God's kingdom regime. You are operating fully within the structure of God's overarching rule.

The definition of a covenant is a divinely created relational bond. Covenants are official, legal, binding, and relational. A covenant is a divinely authorized spiritual structure through which God reveals Himself. It is the key to influencing everything around you for good. God has established the covenant as a governing rule by which He advances His kingdom on earth. In Exodus 19:5-6, God connects all of these concepts we have been looking at in two summary verses. This passage says,

"Now then, if you will indeed obey My voice and keep My covenant, then you shall be My own possession among all the peoples, for all the earth is Mine; and you shall be to Me a kingdom of priests and a holy nation." These are the words that you shall speak to the sons of Israel.

To summarize these two verses, God lets us know that if and when we keep His covenant, then we get to experience the full manifestation of His kingdom. Included in that manifestation are the benefits of the kingdom—such as blessing, provision, power, peace, and so much more.

Keeping God's Covenant

Many people today are not experiencing God's kingdom benefits because they refuse to keep His covenant. Yet God's covenant is a divinely created legal bond, predicated on relationship. For example, marriage is a covenant (Malachi 2:14). The covenant of marriage is a legal relationship whereby two people become bonded together in order to increase the experience of knowing each other. That's why when the Bible introduces the concept of physical intimacy in marriage, it uses the Hebrew word which literally translates into our English term "to know." We read that Adam "knew" Eve, and Eve conceived. This is because the whole point of the relational merge was to enter into a deeper relational experience with the other person.

> *Many people today are not experiencing God's kingdom benefits because they refuse to keep His covenant.*

Thus, when God speaks on covenant and our abiding within His covenant, He is talking about going deeper with Him relationally (Jeremiah

9:23-24) in order to gain access to a greater experience of Him and greater authority from Him. The kingdom covenant within which we are to abide is an enormously big deal. It is a lack of awareness of God's established relational order and His intention of the covenant that prevents a person from fully living out God's destiny and purpose in their life.

Some biblical examples of the covenant that reveal this include the covenants that God made with Abraham, Isaac, Jacob, David, Israel, Palestine, and even the Church in the New Covenant. All throughout the pages of the Bible we read this term: covenant. From Genesis to Revelation, the passages are peppered with the occurrence, reference, or influence of this concept of covenant. It is the rule by which God's kingdom operates as well as allows the broader experience of God confirming and validating His reality as part of our earthly lives.

Like covenants made during Western times or in Western movies when a cowboy and a Native American would cut their hands and share their blood, God says we are establishing an official relationship and accessing the full benefits of His covenant by keeping the commands in His covenant. Yet in the new covenant, the blood has already been shed and shared through Jesus Christ. Our part comes through obedience to His commands. Living within the benefits of the covenant is critical because the covenant provides a covering. It's best explained by the use of an umbrella. When you use an umbrella, you place a covering over your body to protect you from the elements. The umbrella covers you. Now, the umbrella doesn't change the weather. Nor does it stop the rain. But it does cover you so that the rain does not get on you.

A person can have an umbrella and not use the umbrella. If you are holding an umbrella but do not open the umbrella, you are still uncovered.

The reality today is that far too many Christians are in the covenant but the covenantal benefits and covering have been closed to them. Effectively, they are living spiritually uncovered lives. This lack of covering leaves the door open for Satan to have his way with them (Ephesians 4:27). What the enemy wants most is for believers to close their umbrellas, or tuck them away in the garage or some far-off location where they will remain unused and unaccessed. Unfortunately Satan has found a number of ways to get us to do just that.

But when understood and used correctly, the covenant is designed to cover you in such a way that you have the maximum experience of God in your life. As you get to know God more through this unique relational bond, He expresses His pleasure through His presence in your life. The better you come to know God, the more of His covenant you get to experience. As we saw in an earlier chapter where we looked at Moses' desire to know God more than the competing desire to experience God's blessings, knowing God is the foundation of kingdom stewardship. This is a relational role.

As followers of the King and stewards under His care, our relationship with God strengthens and develops as we come to know His desires, likes, dislikes, preferences, and more in a fuller manner.

Thus, the primary focus of a kingdom steward is to know and understand God. Just as men are told to study their wives in order to live out the marriage covenant more fully (1 Peter 3:7), we likewise increase our experience of the covenant when we grow in our understanding and knowledge of God. As a husband develops his ability to discern the various moods, inflections, and looks of his wife, the relationship benefits in intimacy through this increased awareness of and sensitivity to the other. Similarly, as followers of the King and stewards under His care, our relationship with God strengthens and develops as we come to know His desires, likes, dislikes, preferences, and more in a fuller manner.

Aligning under God

I am sure you are aware of what happens when a car gets out of alignment. If this happens to your car, the tires wear unevenly and damage comes at a quicker pace. Not only that, the ride itself becomes shaky. The covenant is God's alignment mechanism whereby when you and I align under His rule in the context of a growing, abiding relationship with Him, we experience the smoothness and protection of His overarching care. When we operate out of alignment with Him and His covenant, our lives get the full effect of uneven wear and tear, as well as the shaking that takes place during times of conflict, chaos, or crisis.

The Bible is clear that the primary goal of the covenant is to deepen your relationship with and experience of God. It's to allow you the realization of a broader involvement of God in your life. Ezekiel 16:62 says, "Thus I will establish My covenant with you, and you shall know that I am the LORD." Knowing God is the foundation of kingdom stewardship.

There is a misconception prevalent in our religious teachings today, and that concerns what exists as the root of our relationship with God. God is not some out-there, distant, cosmic robotic being who hangs the stars in the sky and keeps the oxygen flowing, but cannot relate to our everyday emotions and lacks interest in our lives. No, God is a God of love. The root of our relationship with God is His love. In fact, He loved us before we ever loved Him (1 John 4:19). Deuteronomy 7:7-9 identifies this underlying motivation for God's relationship with us:

> The LORD did not set His love on you nor choose you because
> you were more in number than any of the peoples, for you were
> the fewest of all peoples, but because the LORD loved you and
> kept the oath which He swore to your forefathers, the LORD
> brought you out by a mighty hand and redeemed you from
> the house of slavery, from the hand of Pharaoh king of Egypt.

Know therefore that the LORD your God, He is God, the faithful God, who keeps His covenant and His lovingkindness to a thousandth generation with those who love Him and keep His commandments.

God's covenant is a love thing. He loves you. It's His love that initiated His creation and redemption of mankind. When you lose sight of the driving motivation behind His covenant with you, you limit the movement of the King in your circumstances. You will see His commands as rules to be kept rather than wisdom to protect you. As Scripture states, "For this is the love of God, that we keep His commandments; and His commandments are not burdensome" (1 John 5:3).

— 🌿 —

God's covenant is a love thing. He loves you.

— 🌿 —

Far too many Christians are living lives of defeat because they don't realize God's commandments come from a heart of love. As a result, they operate outside of the covenant. Any time you are functioning apart from complete obedience to God's commands, you are out of alignment. In other words, if what you are doing, saying, or thinking is not what God wants, you are out of alignment with the covenant. It doesn't matter how you choose to justify your actions or words, or even if they make perfect logical sense to you. If what you do and what God says disagree, you're out of alignment with the covenant and, therefore, you're experiencing a diminished relationship with the living God.

Alignment in the structure of the covenant is critical to God confirming and validating His work and kingdom purposes in your life. There exists a causal relationship in covenantal blessings.

Unless you comprehend, believe, and apply that foundational truth to your approach of kingdom stewardship, nothing else I have to say in this book will amount to much more than a hill of beans for you. In fact, if you choose not to believe that foundational truth, you might as well close the book and stick it back on the shelf. Living under the rule of God in His covenantal structure is the primary root of everything else that follows. You cannot operate outside of His commandments and simultaneously operate as a kingdom steward. The two are mutually exclusive. When you function in disobedience to God, you are declaring yourself as the owner and creator of all things in your life. Your prayers will be hindered. Your progress will be thwarted. In fact, your overall peace will disappear.

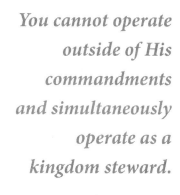

You cannot operate outside of His commandments and simultaneously operate as a kingdom steward.

The Wilderness Experience

You cannot live in rebellion to God and expect God's presence in your life. You might as well start praying to yourself if that is the mindset by which you operate. Because when you establish yourself as king or queen or ruler, then you must look to yourself for provision, protection, peace, blessing, and power. The church can't help you. I can't help you. And God can't help you because He will not accept second place in your life. If you are your own ruler, only you can help you.

When I preached the content of this message to our church in Dallas, I challenged the congregants to read Deuteronomy 8 every day for seven days. That challenge turned into a weekly Bible-reading challenge that has continued to this day where I encourage people to read the same chapter of Scripture every day for a week and ask God for His insight into the Scripture. The purpose of steady engagement in God's Word is to give the Holy Spirit the opportunity to bring more to light for you in your understanding and knowledge of God. Deuteronomy 8 is a great chapter to start with because it contains a tremendously impactful illustration of God's love and our purpose. The context is that the Israelites had come out of Egypt years before on their way to the Promised Land. While on the precipice of entering this land of great expectations, God gave them a review of where they had been.

> *The purpose of steady engagement in God's Word is to give the Holy Spirit the opportunity to bring more to light for you in your understanding and knowledge of God.*

God had delivered them from Egypt. He was taking them to the Promised Land. But in order to get from Egypt to the land flowing with milk and honey, they had to pass through a wilderness first.

We see reminders of His care pop up several times throughout the chapter:

> You shall remember all the way which the LORD your God has led you in the wilderness these forty years, that He might humble you, testing you, to know what was in your heart, whether you would keep His commandments or not.
>
> DEUTERONOMY 8:2

> He led you through the great and terrible wilderness, with its fiery serpents and scorpions and thirsty ground where there was no water; He brought water for you out of the rock of flint.
>
> DEUTERONOMY 8:15

God reminds the Israelites that it was His hand that provided for them when they needed it most. He brought water. He fed them manna. He humbled them so that they would know beyond a shadow of a doubt that He was their Source. Before reaching the blessing, they had to experience the wilderness. They had to come to know God more deeply and more fully in that location that was dry, barren, boring, painful, and undesirable. God will often allow His kingdom stewards a time in the wilderness where they experience dry spells, scorpions, fiery serpents, and lack. In fact, if you have been a Christian for any length of time, I can almost assume you have been through a wilderness experience yourself. These are the seasons where you have to draw close to God or you simply won't make it. You have to follow His lead, eat from His hand, and obey His commands.

The reason God takes each of us through these periods in our lives is revealed in Deuteronomy 8:2. It is so that He can humble us, test us, and develop us that we might remember Him more fully when we enter into that which is abundant and good.

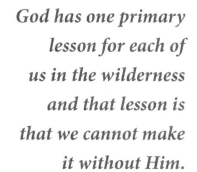

God has one primary lesson for each of us in the wilderness and that lesson is that we cannot make it without Him.

God has one primary lesson for each of us in the wilderness and that lesson is that we cannot make it without Him. God will let you go hungry so that you will know He is your Source. He will let you go thirsty so that you will know He is your Source. He will let things not work out in your favor so that you will know He is your Source. If it weren't for God, none of us would eat, drink, have shoes to wear, or make it into the next moment in time, let alone tomorrow or next week.

The purpose of the wilderness is to position kingdom stewards with the right awareness of God's covenantal design. After all, God knows our propensity to forget. He repeats this twice in Deuteronomy 8: first in verse 11, "Beware that you do not forget the LORD your God," and then in verse 14, "then your heart will become proud and you will forget the LORD your God."

God knows how easy it is for us to assume ownership over what He has given to us. He knows that we will take the credit, if we can, for what He has done. Thus, to remind us that we are entirely dependent upon Him, He allows us to go through the wilderness. He will watch us climb the ladder of self-determination only to then kick the ladder out from under us. Remembrances are very important because they connect us with key events. The key event God seeks to keep us connected with is that He created the world, and we didn't. He provided all we need to exist, and we didn't. He opened the doors of opportunity, and we didn't.

In other words, God owns it all, and we don't own any of it.

Most of us can relate to wanting to take a long nap after a large meal. Especially a meal like Thanksgiving. The energy levels go away when the stomach gets full. Something similar happens in our lives when we get too full of ourselves. When we get the big head, we become spiritually sleepy and no longer remember that all we have and all we are is sourced in God and not us. That's when God has to remind us. He has to allow us to wander in the wilderness for as long as we need until we recognize Him as our Source. The Israelites wandered for forty years. God is patient. He has plenty of time to spare. If you are in a wilderness situation yourself, I recommend aligning your thoughts, words, and actions under His overarching rule.

Acknowledge God as your Source in all that you have. Operate as a manager, not an owner. Then follow His lead. The Israelites turned what could have been a six-week journey to the Promised Land into a forty-year delay because they went year after year after year without learning the lesson of stewardship.

God owns it all, and everything we possess comes from Him (1 Chronicles 29:10-13). Thus, wealth is a spiritual issue and not just an economic one.

None of us are solely dependent on our own human resources. We are all managers entrusted with gifts, skills, time, and ideas to use according to God's leading and His purposes. And yes, God does still provide in the wilderness. He won't leave you high and dry; He sends down manna. And He will usher you into your Promised Land when you surrender to His rule.

God allows the wilderness to humble us because He loves us. He wants a relationship with us. Any kind of relationship with God has to be rooted in truth—the truth that He is the Source and we are entirely dependent upon Him. If you've ever seen a turtle on top of a post, you know that it didn't get there by itself. Somebody much bigger and much stronger than the turtle put it there. We all know that to be true. And yet when businesses boom, churches grow, ministries expand, books sell, podcasts go viral, or anything of that sort seems to happen in our world today, somehow someway we forget the principle of the turtle. Blessing comes from God's hand. And as quickly as He gave it, He can take it away.

God allows the wilderness to humble us because He loves us. He wants a relationship with us.

The wilderness is there to remind you of that. What's more, God won't hesitate to send you through more than one. The lesson is just too important to miss.

The Productive Kingdom Steward

God has established His covenant to prosper us. It is designed for your progression and improvement. God has no intention of bringing you hurt or harm through His covenant. The intention of the covenant is always to help you. Deuteronomy 29:9 emphasizes this truth: "So keep the words of this covenant to do them, that you may prosper in all that you do." Inasmuch as you keep the covenant by operating underneath God's divinely authorized rule as a kingdom steward, you are positioning yourself for God to prosper you.

God is not opposed to your productivity. Deuteronomy 8:18 says clearly, "For it is He who is giving you power to make wealth." God has placed massive potential within His creation. The materials for production and building—all of that comes directly from God Himself. Whatever we make, create, wear, produce, imagine, or dream up is rooted in God. He's blessed us with the mental and physical power to make wealth from His creation. In other words, He's given you the potential to be productive and profitable. All He asks is that you do it according to His directions and overarching rule.

Now, this is not to say that no one prospers financially outside of God's covenant. Many unscrupulous businesses prosper, and even people who have no reflection of God's rule in their lives prosper. But 1 Chronicles 29:12 ties wealth to honor, giving us insight into the fleeting nature of earthly celebrity and riches. We read, "Both riches and honor come from You, and You rule over all, and in Your hand is power and might; and it lies in Your hand to make great and to strengthen everyone."

It's important to remember that God will allow the unrighteous to accumulate wealth so that when the righteous are ready for it, He can transfer it. God will take from the sinner and give it to the saint (Proverbs 13:22). There exist many biblical illustrations of this principle. For example, the Egyptians suffered so greatly under God's judgments against them for not letting the Israelites go, that when the Israelites finally did get set free, the Egyptians gave them gold, silver, and valuables. The former slaves left their captivity wealthy because God transferred the wealth of one group of people to another (Exodus 12:35-36).

When the Israelites entered into the Promised Land, they no longer had any resources of their own. They had been wandering in the wilderness for multiple decades. But God had it already planned out for them. He told them they would inhabit cities they did not build, eat from farms they didn't plant, and profit off the labor and infrastructure that others had previously built (Joshua 24:13).

Another example is when the walls of Jerusalem needed to be rebuilt and Nehemiah, an Israelite, approached the king of Persia to ask for the tools and resources to rebuild it. Essentially, God used a man working for a secular government to gain the finances necessary to rebuild God's city for God's chosen people. The king granted the resources, but what's more, he also granted letters to guarantee safe passage to Nehemiah and others who would oversee the rebuilding process (Nehemiah 2:7-9). I don't want you to get confused when the unrighteous prosper. God has an economic agenda within His kingdom agenda. Nonbelievers can and do become prosperous independently of God but it is a temporary benefit that never ends well (Psalm 73). God has multiple reasons for allowing financial growth, but it is always His rule that governs all. When you abide by His rule and pursue an intimate relationship with Him, He gives you the ability to enjoy what you gain and also to keep it so that it can be used for His purposes.

God's principles of biblical economics apply not only to individuals and families but to societies as well. When the principles are obeyed, people are set free to choose to legitimately maximize their potential for righteous gain. When disobeyed, economic freedom is lost and you wind up with centralized governmental control of the marketplace, which is the evil economic system of the anti-Christ (Revelation 13:16-17).

God's power to produce wealth shows up in many ways. He gives you the power to produce from the supply of His abundant resources. And when you are living covenantally aligned in your knowledge of God and obedience to Him, He plants within you the ideas you need to prosper. In Psalm 25:12-14 we read:

Who is the man who fears the LORD? He will instruct him in the way he should choose. His soul will abide in prosperity, and his descendants will inherit the land. The secret of the LORD is for those who fear Him, and He will make them know His covenant.

God lets kingdom stewards know the secrets to success. He gives you His ideas. When you are aligned relationally with Him, pursuing Him under His covenant, He brings thoughts to you that instruct you on your next steps. It could be things you are thinking of doing, people you are considering speaking to, or places you need to go. Whatever it is, God guides you in the right direction with the right thoughts to do the right things to produce wealth and prosper you if it's His will for you to prosper. I want to bring up the point, though, that there are many faithful and obedient Christians who are not monetarily wealthy. It is never unbiblical to be poor as long as it is not due to laziness, irresponsibility, or oppression. God has a divinely designed destiny for each of us that, with many other variables, will determine our financial status in life.

Friend, you can save a lot of time, energy, frustration, irritation, and all-out mess simply by seeking God.

Friend, you can save a lot of time, energy, frustration, irritation, and all-out mess simply by seeking God. He knows the end from the beginning. He knows what will work and what won't. He will instruct you when you are operating as a kingdom steward under His rule. The power to produce something originates in the thoughts about doing it. Thus, if you can get the right thought, then you can produce the optimal result.

Too many Christians run from these truths because they confuse this with Prosperity Theology. But Prosperity Theology has nothing to do with alignment under God's over-arching rule. It has no connection to the wilderness surrender that comes from recognizing God as your Source. It is a false theology based on human wisdom that produces selfish rebels rather than authentic kingdom stewards. When you are living underneath the covenantal covering and provision of God, that is different from Prosperity Theology. That is Biblical Prosperity. And one key differentiating factor between the two is found in the book of 3 John 1:2: "Beloved,

When you are living underneath the covenantal covering and provision of God, that is different from Prosperity Theology. That is Biblical Prosperity.

I pray that in all respects you may prosper and be in good health, just as your soul prospers."

Now, everybody loves the first part of that verse. Everybody wants their blessing. But when taken in context, this is a prayer that your physical prospering doesn't outpace your spiritual prospering. It is a prayer that your bank account doesn't exceed your spiritual account. It is a prayer that your human resources will not grow larger than your spiritual resources, because if they do, you will forget your Source. You will be sending yourself an invitation to another wilderness experience in order to relearn the foundational principle of life itself: God is the Source of all.

If you love your money, your career, your dreams, or any of your resources more than you love God, then all of those things will be in jeopardy, because all of those things will become subject to God's wilderness reminders.

One of the major problems kingdom stewards run into is not knowing how to spiritually and emotionally manage success. When their success outpaces their spiritual maturity, they run the risk of losing it all. That's why you will often see people make a lot of money, only to lose it or lose the ability to enjoy it. Or people build an enormous business, only to see it go under. God does not desire that His stewards operate in a mindset that leaves Him out and negates His ownership over all they have.

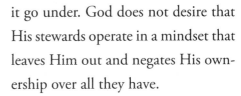

God does not desire that His stewards operate in a mindset that leaves Him out and negates His ownership over all they have.

I've said this before but I really want to encourage you to read Deuteronomy 8 every day until it's practically memorized. This chapter emphasizes the fact over and over again that God is your Source. Everything else is just a resource. You are a steward. You are a manager. God owns everything, and everything He owns is to be used to advance His kingdom. You must be aligned under that, validated by your obedience to Him. Making money or creating success is one thing. Keeping it is another. This is because it is easier to give in to pride when your storehouses are full, and when you give in to pride, you forget this principle: God owns it all and your role as a kingdom steward is to know Him, honor Him, and advance His kingdom in all you do.

When God sees that you are obeying Him because you want to know Him better, then He is free to open up the umbrella of His covenantal care and covering, while simultaneously ushering in the floods of His blessings. When he sees that you and I are gratefully prioritizing His divinely bestowed resources to advance His kingdom agenda in history, then He finds pleasure in giving us additional ideas and strategies to expand our productivity and profitability (Isaiah 48:17). That is what it means to live your life as a kingdom steward. When you can understand the importance of the covenant, you will have unlocked the secret to emotional, physical, spiritual, and financial success.

When you buy an appliance, it comes with a manufacturer's warranty. The warranty states that the manufacturer will stand behind the product if something doesn't work out. The manufacturer will replace the product or fix the product if it breaks due to a malfunction of the product. But there is always a proviso in the warranty. This proviso states that if you use the product for something other than what it was created for, you invalidate the warranty. In such a case, you lose the rights of repair, restoration, or replacement.

God has a warranty for your life. If you are a believer who has placed your faith in Christ alone for the forgiveness of your sins, He has warrantied your existence. This warranty even comes with a covenantal guarantee. But the assumption tied to this warranty is that you are stewarding your life for the purposes established by the Creator. You are using your time, talents, and treasures for His covenant, His kingdom, and His glory. The moment you start operating behind enemy lines or against the intentions of the Manufacturer's specifications, you are invalidating the warranty. Many people wonder why their prayers aren't answered. They wonder why they lack peace. They wonder why they aren't

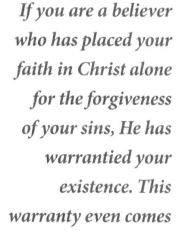

If you are a believer who has placed your faith in Christ alone for the forgiveness of your sins, He has warrantied your existence. This warranty even comes with a covenantal guarantee.

experiencing the benefits of God's grace. But the answer is simple: They have messed up the warranty. They have come out from under God's covering when they have chosen to live their lives according to their own will and purposes, not according to God's.

If this is you, there is hope. Even if you are in the wilderness right now because you've been building your own personal kingdom, you can return. You can come back underneath the covering of God by repenting of your sin of independence and by passionately prioritizing pursuing Him, knowing Him, and aligning your thoughts, words, and actions within the structure of His covenantal rule. When you do, He will begin the process of fulfilling the warranty of your life from this day forward.

5

SPHERES

If you were to come to my house and pull out a cigarette, I would ask you to take your cigarette outside. For starters, I don't have ashtrays in my house. Second, we don't allow smoking in our home.

If you came over for an afternoon of fellowship and took out a bottle of Jack Daniel's from your back pocket, my wife and I would ask you, out of respect for it being our home, to put it away. We don't condone the drinking of hard liquor and so we don't allow it in our house.

If you stopped by our house to say hello and started to use profanity as you spoke, we would speak up to ask you to refrain from swearing because one of the rules of our house is that we do not allow profanity.

Now, those are just some of the rules at our house. There are more. But that gives you an idea. The reason we can make rules like that is because it's our house. I'm sure you have governing guidelines for what takes place in your house as well. There's nothing unusual about that. But I'm also sure that if you have ever been a parent of teenagers, there were times when your kids sought to bring the rules of other people's homes into your house. They may have told you about these other rules and explained how they worked in other homes, all the while seeking to establish standards from elsewhere in your domain.

My kids did that as well. There were many times as they were growing up that we would have to explain to them that what they proposed simply wasn't how we did things in our house. Of course, they would ask, "Why?" To which I would reply, "Because it's our house." You wouldn't be surprised to hear that a conflict would inevitably arise if they insisted on someone else's rules in our house. That conflict was short-lived because they did not have the jurisdiction to insist on anything at all.

We live in God's house. He calls His house the kingdom. The primary, overarching rule in God's house is that He reigns. He claims ownership and, as such, He has established the rules for how His house is supposed to work. Now, "rules" may be a harsh term and one that some people balk at. After all, aren't we simply called to love God and love others (through the New Covenant)? Yes, we are. Yet, within the calling to love God and love others are prescribed methods, approaches, attitudes, and more that define and express that love. For the sake of this illustration, I'm referring to all of these as "rules."

> *We live in a day when people are borrowing rules from society that do not agree with the rules of the owner.*

Unfortunately, some kids have come into His house with a new set of rules. They have decided there are rules of His they don't care for. So, they've chosen to bring in other rules and other standards—standards set by Satan and his rival kingdom. The only problem is, they have done this in God's house. And just as happens with our own kids when they seek to bring other rules into our homes, conflicts erupt between the owner and the resident when standards are not aligned.

We live in a day when people are borrowing rules from society that do not agree with the rules of the owner. They are spending an inordinate amount of time gleaning rules from talk radio, reality shows, entertainment, and social media. This "babble-by-the-hour" has permeated the worldview of our society so much that it has become difficult to even recognize the presence of Christian values in our culture. Truth has been undermined. Everyone has their own version of truth. This used to be known as opinions, but somehow each person is now entitled to formulating their own set of truths by which to live. This has happened many times throughout history and it never ends up good (see Judges 21:25).

It's only when we abide by and operate under the structure of God's overarching rule that we will experience the benefits of His blessings and favor in our lives. Knowing and understanding His rules is the first step toward following them, so in this chapter I want to take a look at the four covenantal stewardship spheres within which God has organized the expression of His rule. Psalm 128 summarizes these four spheres of God's covenantal expression, breaking down His rule into its irreducible minimum. No area of your life sits outside these four realms. Remember that a covenant is a divinely created relational bond. It's an official agreement arranged and established by God through which His kingdom values are to be understood, yielded to, and followed. There's one more thing you must understand before we look at these four covenantal stewardship spheres. At some point there will be a big payday where you will receive a reward for how you managed life in these realms. We see the reference to the results of proper management pop up time and again in this passage of Psalm 128. It shows up as the word "blessed." We read:

How blessed is everyone who fears the LORD. (verse 1)
Behold, for thus shall the man be blessed. (verse 4)
The LORD bless you from Zion. (verse 5)

To speak of a blessing is to speak of divine favor. A blessing includes experiencing, enjoying, and extending the goodness of God in your life. The act of obtaining blessings in your life is directly tied to how well you manage or steward what God has entrusted you with.

Far too many people want God to bless them while they go about changing the rules in His house. They seek divine favor all the while piggybacking on the rules of the enemy. Praying for a blessing does not equate to receiving that blessing. Blessings are frequently tied to your alignment under God's rule. As a matter of fact, the word "bless" in Psalm 128 is directly tied to operating within your managerial responsibility according to God's will. When you truly grasp that truth, and apply it to how you think, decide, and react, you will begin to witness the favor of God showing up in four covenantal spheres of your life like you never even imagined He would.

> *To speak of a blessing is to speak of divine favor. A blessing includes experiencing, enjoying, and extending the goodness of God in your life.*

The four spheres of stewardship mentioned in Psalm 128 are the individual, the family, the church, and the community, and each sphere has an economic benefit to it when it operates properly underneath God's kingdom rule. Let's look at each of them in the remainder of this chapter.

Sphere 1—The Individual

Proper kingdom stewardship begins with your personal life. You must own His truth. In fact, God Himself starts with you. We read at the beginning of Psalm 128 that He addresses personal stewardship first. Verses 1-2 say,

How blessed is everyone who fears the LORD, who walks in His ways. When you shall eat of the fruit of your hands, you will be happy and it will be well with you.

God starts with you. When you have aligned yourself under God's authority, all else will fall into place. I know it's easy to focus on other people and what they are doing or how they are acting or how they may even be getting on your nerves. But all you ultimately control is yourself. Your first responsibility as God's steward is to fear God. It's not to point out what other people are doing wrong. It's not to bemoan the challenges in life. It's not to promote yourself in your own personal brand or platform. No, your first and primary responsibility as a steward is to fear God.

I like to explain the concept of fearing God simply as taking Him seriously. It doesn't mean to run in fright, cower in shame, or hide from His heavy hand. Fearing, in this case and throughout the Bible when referencing God, has to do with reverencing God. Obeying Him. Honoring Him. Taking Him seriously.

Very few people truly fear God in today's culture. Marginalizing and dismissing Him has become a way of life for far too many, even for far too many churches. We live in a culture that takes God casually. He's good for the invocation and the benedictions, as long as He stays out of everything in between. He's good for grace before a meal, as long as He doesn't interrupt the activities throughout the day. He's good for a few moments of devotional thought in the morning or evening, as long as He doesn't interfere with the rest of our thoughts.

Your first responsibility as God's steward is to fear God.

We live in a day with God on discount. He's marked down for quick-sale. Sure, people want God as long as they can get God cheap. By cheap, I mean no commitment, investment, saving, or sacrifice on their end. It's a dime-store God on discount that people seek today. As soon as He comes at full price, they'll shop elsewhere.

People want the benefits of eternity while making independent decisions in time. They want to instruct the Owner on how they ought to live their lives. They want to use God without respecting Him.

We all have electricity in our homes. I want to give you a warning about that electricity that you probably already know: You'd better take it seriously. You can benefit from it, enjoy it, warm yourself by it—but don't go sticking a screwdriver into an outlet. As soon as you disrespect the rules of electricity, you will pay the price for breaking those rules. Electricity will light you up, serving notice that it must be taken seriously at all times, by all people.

God is not a spare tire to be kept in the vicinity in case life goes flat. He's not a slot machine whose lever you pull in order to hear the clinking of the blessing. God is God. He is Ruler. Creator. King. And not taking Him seriously goes against everything He has told us about Himself in His Word. Psalm 128 makes it clear that His favor is tied to our fear of Him.

So how do you know if you fear God? How do you know that you aren't merely talking a good game? How can you discern that this relationship is truly real for you and not just religion? The first verse of Psalm 128 says it's because you are walking in His ways. A person fears God with their feet, not just with their feelings. They fear God with their movement, not just with their mouth. It's your walk, not just your talk. You fear God with your life, not just your lips. If you ever are unsure about whether you take God seriously, just look at the direction of your feet. When you walk according to His ways, you fear Him. When you don't, you don't. An obvious contradiction exists between fearing God and moving in the opposite direction of His revealed will.

Fearing God shows up in your decision-making because your decisions affect your movement. If what you do and what God says oppose each other, then it is obvious that you do not fear God. You do not take Him seriously. You take Him casually. You may want enough of God to look and sound spiritual, but not enough to actually be spiritual. When you are not in concert with what He says, you're just talking noise. And it's true that you may even be fooling people, but you won't be fooling God. Last I checked, He's the only One who dispenses eternal blessings and favor.

If what you do and what God says oppose each other, then it is obvious that you do not fear God. You do not take Him seriously.

A person who walks in God's ways, connects with Him authentically, pursues Him passionately, and aligns under Him fully has positioned themselves for His favor.

God is not against blessings. He is not against giving favor. He is against spiritual blessings and favor for those who are acting contrary to and independently of His will. He says that if you will execute the carrying out of His plans according to His Word—that's when you will see Him show up. Movement invokes blessing.

This is similar to the motion-detector lighting we have installed throughout the church where I pastor. We installed these because too many people were leaving the lights on and running up the electricity bill. Now the lights only come on when the sensor detects movement. The power responds to purpose.

That doesn't mean we took out the lights. The lights are in the room. The power is in the room. But now they have been programmed not to express themselves until movement is detected. Similarly, God's power is programmed through His universal truths not to manifest itself until He sees the motion of obedience and reverence in our lives. That's why you can see all throughout the Bible that before God would do something supernatural, He would tell people to do something first. He instructed Moses to hold out the rod. He told Joshua that the priests would need to put their feet in the Jordan River. He told Martha to move the stone. All of these things had to be done "first" because God responds to obedience carried out in faith. And He responds graciously.

Psalm 128:1-2 tells us there is a threefold reward for fearing God. First, "You shall eat of the fruit of your hands." That refers to your labor. When you steward all of life according to His rules, you will witness God joining you in your work. You'll experience God blessing you in your career. You'll receive His favor on the job. To "eat of the fruit of your hands" means to enjoy the benefits of what you have worked for. Rather than live paycheck to paycheck as if your bank account is a bag filled with holes, God will guide you in how you spend your income and He will bless you in the use of it.

Second, God says that when you fear Him, you "will be happy." You will receive the reward of happiness. Happiness is that far-too-often elusive state of being which produces calm, peace, and overall enjoyment. Absent in happiness are emotions such as worry, anxiety, jealousy, pride, and disapproval. Things will go well with your state of mind. God will be working things out one, two, or ten steps ahead of you so that as you walk into them, they have already been prepared. In fact, for those who fear him, He's working things out next year that you can't even anticipate this year. When you take God seriously, He is out in front of what you do, smoothing the way for you.

Third, "It will be well with you." This speaks about God covering your future.

One of the amazing things about God is that we rarely even see what He is doing. He is so far ahead of us and so far above our thinking that He is tweaking and maneuvering things for our best intended outcome without us even realizing it. When you take Him seriously in the day-to-day decisions of life, He takes your future seriously in His plans and preparations.

Sphere 2—The Family

The next sphere God has given us to steward is the family. We read in Psalm 128:3-4,

> Your wife shall be like a fruitful vine within your house, your children like olive plants around your table. Behold, for thus shall the man be blessed who fears the LORD.

The husband's stewardship is mentioned here, and it is a role that I have not seen enough husbands actively live out. Unfortunately, our minds have been tainted as to the role of biblical manhood in that far too many men believe that we are to be as productive as we can, while our wives are only there to support us. Yet this verse clearly says that it is the role of the husband to make his wife as productive as she can be. A fruitful vine symbolizes growth, production, and even provision. Thus, the man is to steward his family by overseeing their well-being in a way that encourages the expression of personal gifts and talents.

The role of a husband is to shape the spiritual productivity and growth of his wife and children.

The breakdown of the family is one of the major social crises of our day. It has produced poverty, abandonment, increased crime, mental and emotional issues, and stagnant souls. Largely responsible for this is the redefining of family by men. Men, you are a thermostat. Your job is not to respond. Your job is to set the temperature. If there are issues in your home—with your wife or with your children—look to God and then yourself to fix them. Look within. Your family reflects the love and care (or lack of love and care) you give them. Don't expect a summer wife if you bring home winter weather.

For a vine to produce fruit, it must be diligently cared for. Yes, there will be thorns, thistles, and weeds at some point. But it's the responsibility of the man leading the family to remove the weeds and tend to the vine so that it grows, flourishes, and produces. The role of a husband is to shape the spiritual productivity and growth of his wife and children. The role of a wife is to encourage and support the spiritual productivity and growth of her husband and children. God told us clearly in this passage that the wife is to be a fruitful vine in her home. That doesn't mean she is not to work outside of the home. But what it does mean is that her home must never be secondary to her commitment to her career, platform,

The role of a wife is to encourage and support the spiritual productivity and growth of her husband and children.

podcast, blog, or brand. A wife's commitment in facilitating the home and honoring the one who is to make her a fruitful vine (her husband) is to always come first. A wife's stewardship enhances the productivity of her husband (Proverbs 31:23).

Ladies, your husband should feel your honor. He should rest easy in your respect. He should know that if and when he needs you—you are there. When the relationship between husband and wife reflects God's rule, the children will be like olive plants around the table.

The only way an olive plant can become an olive tree is if its roots run deep. But we have a generation of unrooted kids because parents haven't focused on tending to their roots. We have a misguided, entitled group of young adults who balk at the wisdom of those older than them because they distrusted the actions of their parents when they were raised.

Parents are called by God to steward their families around the table. We are to use the table time not only as a place where we eat together but also as a place where parents can minister, guide, bless, correct, mentor, encourage, and train their children in kingdom values.

But it seems like families today are no longer around the table. Instead, they are around the television. Or around the smartphones. Or not even eating together at all. Thus, the culture is getting to invest, influence, and impact more in our children than we are as parents.

God has called each of us who has children to steward the atmosphere and direction of the home. If you have a family, you have a primary responsibility to raise your "olive plants" to become productive olive trees since olives were used in a myriad of social, medicinal, spiritual, and economically beneficial ways.

> *We are to use the table time not only as a place where we eat together but also as a place where parents can minister, guide, bless, correct, mentor, encourage, and train their children in kingdom values.*

Sphere 3—The Church

The third sphere you are to manage in God's covenantal structure is that of the church. We read in Psalm 128:5,

The LORD bless you from Zion.

Zion is a lofty word that describes God's holy dwelling place. It was known by several terms such as Mount Zion, the City of Zion, and even the Temple called Zion. Whether it is the mountain, city, or temple, it indicated the space in which God's manifest presence dwelt. In this passage, the psalmist is writing about the temple. We know this because he moves on to talk about the city at a later point. The temple was a place of worship. Worship is the recognition of God for who He is, what He has done, and what you are trusting Him to do. It involves the celebration of God. Those in Zion also set the standards that were to infiltrate the culture. Zion was to set the agenda for society at large.

All of this began with the recognition of the true God. When the church fails in teaching the principles and precepts of the one true God, chaos ensues. We read in 2 Chronicles 15:3-6:

> For many days Israel was without the true God and without a teaching priest and without law. But in their distress they turned to the LORD God of Israel, and they sought Him, and He let them find Him. In those times there was no peace to him who went out or to him who came in, for many disturbances afflicted all the inhabitants of the lands. Nation was crushed by nation, and city by city, for God troubled them with every kind of distress.

When there is no teaching priest, no law, and no true God, the result is conflict. Conflict is inevitable when God is not presented properly in the culture. Conflict shows up in individual lives, families, communities, and nations. We are experiencing this today. We live in the dumbing-down of God in our society. But the reason we live in the dumbing-down of God in our society is because the church has also chosen the path of dumbing-down God in Zion. Because we have reduced His significance and voice within the church walls, society has merely reflected our lead in reducing His significance and voice elsewhere. Gatherings on Sunday have turned into nothing more than huddles in a football game. The huddle does nothing to improve the score of the game. It's only when the players break the huddle and carry out the play that they stand a chance of forward progress.

Can you imagine what would happen at the Super Bowl if all the two teams chose to do was huddle? You would have angry coaches, fans, spectators, advertisement agencies, and more. Teams don't aspire to huddle well. They aspire to play well and win. But far too often in our contemporary Christian culture, we aim only to huddle well. We gather together for small group fellowship, outings, and activities but do very little in advancing God's kingdom down the field of play. And while there is nothing wrong with fellowship and activities, what it seems we have forgotten is that they aren't the only things necessary for living all of life as a kingdom steward.

Worship is the recognition of God for who He is, what He has done, and what you are trusting Him to do. It involves the celebration of God.

When God established the temple, it became a place of worship for all of His people. It was the central hub of life itself. It wasn't just a stop on a long list of errands to run. It wasn't intended to be drive-through Christianity. Or convenience-store religion. Zion existed as the starting point from which all else would extend.

I played football every weekend that I could as a teenager. Knowing the chores that were awaiting me when I got home, I would always enter the house talking a little more loudly than normal. "Oh, boy," I would say after walking through the front door. "I am so tired. Wow, I am just beat. I think I will go upstairs and rest!" The translation of those statements meant that I wasn't really wanting to be bothered or asked to do anything around the house.

My mom never gave in though. She would always reply just as loudly, if not even more so, "You'd better get yourself up off that bed and help in this house!" Even when I would resist, she wouldn't give in. "I'm tired," I'd say, hoping this was the day she would let me rest. But no. Her words came fast and heavy, "Did you just tell me you're tired?" She didn't really expect me to answer that question. I knew that by how quickly she went into the next statement, "Let me tell you something about being tired. If not being tired was a criterion to function, then your breakfast would not be made, your lunch would not be made, and your clothes would not be clean. In fact, if not being tired was a requirement to function, I would have gotten rid of you the day after you were born!"

In other words, certain things just demand responsibility. You can't experience all the benefits of the house and not bring any effort to the keeping of the house. This is critical to comprehend because your blessings are tied to your involvement in God's kingdom agenda. They do not automatically come to you just because you are a Christian. God wants you investing in the lives of His other saints, not just asking Him to bless you.

We gather together for small group fellowship, outings, and activities but do very little in advancing God's kingdom down the field of play.

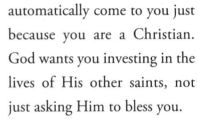

Too many church members are sticking their thumbs out for a free ride these days. We live in a day of spiritual hitchhikers. And once they are done with one church, they just hop over to another. Our churches no longer have sturdy wooden doors on them. They have been replaced with revolving doors. But to be disconnected from the local church is to lose out on a greater level of divine favor that would otherwise be available to you, and this includes economic benefits (Acts 4:32-37; 2 Corinthians 9:6-12;

Philippians 4:15-19). This is not how God intended His church to operate. We read of her glory in Hebrews 12:22-23, "But you have come to Mount Zion and to the city of the living God, the heavenly Jerusalem, and to myriads of angels, to the general assembly and church of the firstborn who are enrolled in heaven, and to God, the Judge of all, and to the spirits of the righteous made perfect."

When you come to Zion, as a kingdom steward, where the presence of God is dwelling in the collective gathering of His church body, you come to serve by stewarding the time, talents, and treasures He's entrusted you with.

When you come to Zion, as a kingdom steward, where the presence of God is dwelling in the collective gathering of His church body, you come to serve by stewarding the time, talents, and treasures He's entrusted you with. You've come to study, practice, and then go teach His precepts concerning His governing kingdom authority. When you do, this verse says that blessing awaits you.

Sphere 4—The Community

The fourth covenantal sphere through which God carries out His kingdom rule is found in the city and country, more broadly known as the community, which includes government. We read in Psalm 128:5-6:

> And may you see the prosperity of Jerusalem all the days of your life. Indeed, may you see your children's children. Peace be upon Israel!

I recently led a tour of around seven hundred people to Israel. Out of all the places we visited, Jerusalem stood out. So much history rests within the walls of that great city. As we drove around the city wall on our way to one of the destinations, I asked our guide about crime and poverty. I hadn't seen anything that indicated either was present. Our guide explained that both of those communal issues were rarely experienced in Jerusalem. The city had structured itself in such a way as to alleviate them.

His words took me to this passage—a passage of promise and prosperity for Jerusalem. But the passage doesn't only speak of Jerusalem, it also speaks of generational impact and the peace of the entire nation. We have another word we often use today to signify generational impact. We call it legacy.

Prosperity. Legacy. Peace. These are the results of a person, family, and church who fear God and function in alignment as kingdom stewards under His overarching rule.

As I enter into this season of my ministry—now in my seventh decade of life—legacy has come to mean more to me than ever before. There's something about aging that puts life's achievements and ambitions in perspective. So much of what we chase when we are younger revolves around the immediate. But as we grow in wisdom, we seek to leave substantial blessings behind for those who come after us.

Prosperity. Legacy. Peace. These are the results of a person, family, and church who fear God and function in alignment as kingdom stewards under His overarching rule.

Yet it doesn't take a genius to see that we lack prosperity, legacy, and peace comprehensively in our nation. Yes, some people prosper but many do not. A few leave a legacy but most do not. Peace is elusive to nearly everyone who isn't on vacation at that moment in time. We are, in short, a nation in turmoil. We face political turmoil, social turmoil, racial turmoil, gender turmoil, economic turmoil, and much more. But none of that should come as a surprise. Because as we read earlier in 2 Chronicles 15:3-6, when God is excluded from the order and rule of a land, chaos erupts.

In my Tony Evans translation, God calls out to us, "You are in a hot mess because I am not in the vicinity! I've been dismissed from your lives, kicked out of your schools, set on the sidelines of your churches, removed from your homes, and marginalized in your culture. You've excluded Me, so conflict abounds!"

When God's presence is no longer felt, the vacuum must be filled.

Often it is filled with chaos.

Thus, the challenge today is for Christians to take their faith public. We are to no longer live as secret-agent believers or spiritual CIA representatives. It is time that we take the values of our King and His kingdom into all areas of our lives—including our community, city, and country. To do less is to fail as a kingdom steward. Far too many believers, if they were accused of being a follower of Jesus Christ, would be found innocent of all charges. That cannot be. We have been called to leave an impact on our culture. Jeremiah 29:7 says that we are to "seek the welfare of the city where I have sent you into exile, and pray to the LORD on its behalf; for in its welfare you will have welfare.'"

The challenge today is for Christians to take their faith public. We are to no longer live as secret-agent believers or spiritual CIA representatives.

The presence of God's people in a community should have a major spiritual, social, and economic impact on the people around them through their good works. Jeremiah 29:4-6 makes it clear that this impact comes through economic development, family stability, and a better social order as God's people pray for, model, and implement kingdom values in the secular environment in which they find themselves. In other words, if the church is doing what it has been called to do, our communities, cities, and nation should become better places to live, work, and raise families. There must be community impact. It's not an option. There must be local and national influence. It's not a request. We are to invest in the well-being of those around us and pray on their behalf as we function as salt and light in the world (Matthew 5:13-16).

— ✿ —

If the church is doing what it has been called to do, our communities, cities, and nation should become better places to live, work, and raise families.

— ✿ —

Out of necessity, having a community perspective involves impacting the institution of civil government, which was created by God to maintain a safe, just, righteous, and compassionate environment in order for freedom to flourish (Romans 13:1-7). Since civil government has a direct effect on its citizens, it is critical that kingdom stewards leverage their spiritual, social, economic, and educational influence to promote a biblical view of government. The goal is for us to live in an orderly society that protects religious freedom (1 Timothy 2:1-4).

If we aren't seeing people saved, environments changed, and errant worldviews challenged and corrected, we are failing as kingdom stewards. God has placed these realms under our authority to manage well. To do any less is to neglect our calling and purpose.

You and I are God's representatives in history. We are to wield His influence in the lives of others. We are not the salt in the shaker. We are the salt of the earth. Nor are we the light of the lamp. We are the light of the world. That's why it is absolutely critical that you learn to look at all of life as a steward. If God could have found ten righteous people in the towns of Sodom and Gomorrah, those towns would still be on the map. Just ten. I want to encourage you to be one of the ten in your town today. If there's more than ten, great. Leave that in God's hands. But as far as it depends on you, be one.

You can start by aligning your life within these four realms of covenantal stewardship. First, God must be allowed to rule your individual life. That means you will check for His decision and thoughts on a matter before you make your decision so that you align under Him. Second, you will shepherd your family according to His will. Third, you will actively engage in the productivity and ministry of your local church. Fourth, you will use the platform and position God has given you in the community to bring His values and viewpoint to bear.

God must be first. First in your life. First in your home. First in your church. First in your community and country. And where He is not first, it's your job to try to change that. You fight for your family. You fight for your marriage. You go to war for your children. You become an engaged part of a local church and fight for it to become strong. You fight for collective impact. As a kingdom citizen, you fight to let your community and country know that Jesus Christ is Lord. Kingdom stewards are not ashamed of the gospel. We are not ashamed of our faith. And, yes, while we need to share God's truth with a spirit of love and an emphasis on clarity, we do need to share it.

You and I have a charge to keep and that charge is to glorify God. We will do just that when we choose to steward our lives, families, churches,

> *God must be first. First in your life. First in your home. First in your church. First in your community and country.*

and the well-being of the community and country in which we live, work, and play. As we learn to navigate under God in these covenantal spheres as kingdom stewards, we invite a greater expression of His presence and power into all we do. Additionally, we experience the spiritual, social, and economic stability and advancement that God intends for society through the presence of His people who are faithfully functioning as His kingdom stewards.

6

STRATEGY

When my son Jonathan was young, we launched our church youth basketball league. I would frequently take him to the games. Of course, he was just starting out and learning the art of playing basketball at the time so some games were better than others. I remember one of Jonathan's games in particular because of something unusual that happened at this game.

Both teams were at mid-court. A player on the opposing team was passing the ball to a teammate when Jonathan came between the two boys and stole the ball. Jonathan then dribbled the ball and went up for a layup with no one defending him. Usually someone tries to run down and defend the layup, or at least look like they are running down. But Jonathan was the only one at the basket. All the other players pretty much stopped at mid-court. The reason they stopped was because Jonathan put the ball in the wrong team's basket. He scored points that the other team got credit for because while he may have been working hard to get them, he wound up in the wrong place.

One of the primary principles of the game of basketball is that you only get the points that go in your team's basket. Thus, the strategy of basketball is to score in your own basket. Similarly, kingdom stewards only advance God's kingdom agenda and bring Him glory when they live according to His purposes. Not their own.

Hard work isn't always the key to spiritual success. In fact, it seems these days that hard work has become its own idol. "Busy" is the new status-symbol for our culture, as I mentioned earlier. But if you and I are busy about the wrong things—instead of strategically advancing God's kingdom—the enemy gets the points. And all we get is God looking at us and asking what on earth we are doing.

Many followers of Jesus Christ are guilty of dunking balls in the wrong basket. We've got an army of spiritual busy-bees, activities, programs, social media sites, podcasts, platforms, small groups, and much more—but the depth of our spiritual impact seems to be waning rather than increasing over time. One of the reasons this is true rests in this area of kingdom stewardship. As we have seen throughout this book, every area of a person's life belongs to God. We are gifted our time, talents, and treasures for the simple purpose of managing them for God's purposes.

But far too many people have gotten this concept backwards. They believe that they own all they have and that God is a distant bystander unless needed in a crisis or emergency. In that mindset, they shoot basket after basket with no one defending them because why would the opposing team defend layups being shot in their own basket?

The Shrewd Steward

Jesus tells a parable in Luke 16 that gives us insight into how important understanding and applying a biblical strategy of effective stewardship is to God. It's a good lesson that Jesus shares in this story, even though it is about a bad man. The audience Jesus told this parable to was His disciples, but as we see later on in the passage, there were Pharisees listening in nearby. In fact, they are referred to as "lovers of money" in verse 14. Jesus sought to make a point using a context they could comprehend.

The main character in the parable is called an unrighteous steward. Regardless of the steward's motivation, Jesus still highlights his strategy as a life lesson for those who were listening to Him at that time. As well as a life lesson for each of us.

The key details in the story found in Luke 16:1-13 can be summarized in this way. There are two main characters—an owner and a manager. The manager oversees the business dealings of the owner. He lives on the owner's property. We know that because he winds up needing to find another house when he loses his job. The manager had been entrusted with everything. He engages with all of the owner's assets. He might be considered a business manager, in our contemporary culture.

Now, over time someone reports to the owner that the manager has been ripping him off. The manager is making bad deals, losing the owner money and failing in his task of seeking productive growth for the owner. In fact, the biblical text goes so far as to say that this manager was found to be "squandering" the owner's assets.

Thus, the owner calls the manager in for a meeting. In this meeting he tells him that he has examined the bookkeeping and has come to the conclusion that the manager has not only misused his role, he's abused it. He's lost money for the owner, wasted his time, and caused the business to decrease in value rather than increase in value—which had been his assigned task. Needless to say, the manager got fired. This man is now without a job. So that puts him in a catch-22 because by this time, he's too old for manual labor. He's too proud to beg. But he needs a place to live and he needs food to eat. Unless the man comes up with a strategy really quick, he's about to find himself on the streets.

So that's exactly what he does. He has an idea. By going to the owner's business clients who are in a position of owing the owner debts, he can work out a deal in his favor. We read about this in verses 5-7:

And he summoned each one of his master's debtors, and he began saying to the first, "How much do you owe my master?" And he said, "A hundred measures of oil." And he said to him, "Take your bill, and sit down quickly and write fifty." Then he said to another, "And how much do you owe?" And he said, "A hundred measures of wheat." He said to him, "Take your bill, and write eighty."

Obviously, the man had enough clout to reduce each bill. And he chose to use it while he still had the chance. Now, you might think this is an unusual story to wind up in the Bible. It's not the typical parable we read. But as we look closely at the owner's response to the manager, and how Jesus emphasizes this response, it becomes even more unexpected.

Because not only did the owner go against many of our natural inclinations of locking the manager in jail until he paid back the reduced debts, but the owner actually praised the man's shrewdness and strategy. It says, "And his master praised the unrighteous manager because he had acted shrewdly; for the sons of this age are more shrewd in relation to their own kind than the sons of light" (verse 8).

Jesus went on to use this example as a teaching point when He said,

And I say to you, make friends for yourselves by means of the wealth of unrighteousness, so that when it fails, they will receive you into the eternal dwellings. He who is faithful in a very little thing is faithful also in much; and he who is unrighteous in a very little thing is unrighteous also in much. Therefore if you have not been faithful in the use of unrighteous wealth, who will entrust the true riches to you? And if you have not been faithful in the use of that which is another's, who will give you that which is your own?

LUKE 16:9-12

Jesus' point to His disciples and to the Pharisees standing around was that the sons of this age were often more strategically shrewd than the sons of light. Sinners know better than saints how to cut the right deal. Sinners know better than saints how to take advantage of an opportunity through the use of earth's resources and personal relationships in order to get ahead in business. Sinners know better than saints how to protect and provide for their future. Even though the owner calls the manager unrighteous, he simultaneously praises the manager. So, while the manager was wrong in what he did, he was smart in how he reversed his situation. He came up with a plan to cause his future to be brighter than his past, and that plan was nothing short of strategic.

In business terms, the manager transmuted the debt. Transmutation is a term that means you take something and turn it into something else because you believe the thing you turn it into will pay larger dividends in the long run. For example, when a person buys a piece of property, that person is transmuting dollars for land. But the only reason they transmute dollars for land is because they believe the appreciation of the land over time is going to be more valuable than the dollars it cost to get it in the first place. Or if a person invests in a start-up company, that person believes the growth of the company will return a greater profit than the original amount invested.

What the owner saw in the manager's activities impressed him. Even though the man stole from him. Even though the man wasted his profits by cutting deals. The owner said he had to give him credit that he was, in fact, shrewdly strategic. While the manager could not change the past, he could change the future.

Now, I know that there are many people reading this book who have found themselves in as drastic and hopeless a situation as this manager did. Perhaps you are one of them. You may have squandered time in the past. Or maybe you squandered talents in the past. Or you've wasted resources God gave you to manage and oversee. And, like the man in the parable, you are staring into your future—and even into eternity—with little or nothing to show for yourself. You may not even know how you are going to successfully navigate your future at all. In short, you have not been a good kingdom steward.

But Jesus offers wisdom to us all in this parable. He offers us a strategy of recovery. Now, I want to clarify that we are not being instructed to copy the unjust steward's actions: We can't endorse wrong actions. We are, however, being warned that to live without a strategy is to live foolishly. It is akin to scoring points in the opposing team's basket. More than that, to live without a mindset of our future is also to live foolishly.

Thus, to anyone who looks onto the horizon and sees nothing but desert sand, He shows us in this story that you can have a brighter future than your past has prepared for you. It may take some insight and strategy. It will definitely take investments of some sort. But there is a way to overcome the mess you may have made in your history and turn it into something else that pays dividends in your eternal future.

This is exactly what the shrewd manager did. He overcame the mess he had created by investing in a way that would provide him with a stable future. By cutting the debtors a great deal, this man knew that they would then welcome him into their homes in the future. They would also be favorable to him later when he lost his job. His shrewdness provided an opportunity for his comeback.

Keep in mind that Jesus is talking to His disciples in telling this parable. Yes, the Pharisees can overhear Him, but His point is directed at His own disciples. These are Christians whom Jesus is encouraging to be shrewd. We read earlier in verse 9 that Jesus instructed them to make friends by virtue of the wealth of unrighteousness so that when it fails (which it will), they will receive you into eternal dwellings.

Here's what you need to know: Jesus is telling you and me to cover our future (both earthly and eternal) through our strategic decisions in our present. We are to invest in our future by strategically operating in our present environment. One day money is going to fail you. For example, if the doctor says a person has a terminal illness, money cannot change that. Money can't bail a person out of everything. There will always be situations in your life that money can't buy a person out of. Eventually, it loses its power. It loses its potency. It loses its ability to resolve the problems. Or it simply runs out or is destroyed (2 Peter 3:10). If you put all of your eggs in the money basket, you will eventually find yourself in a lot of trouble and without any resources when money fails.

> *We are to invest in our future by strategically operating in our present environment.*

This reminds me of a humorous story told about a doctor, a pastor, and a lawyer. All three of these men knew another man who was terminally ill. The man called all three professionals to him and told them, "I don't have much longer to live so here's what I'm going to do. I'm going to give $10,000 to you as my doctor, $10,000 to my pastor, and another $10,000 to you as my lawyer. But when I die, I want each of you to put that $10,000 in my casket so that I will have $30,000 in my casket when I'm buried."

Not too long after that meeting the man died. They held his funeral according to plan and each of the three professionals went by his casket and placed something in it. After the funeral, the three men got together to talk about the man and his funeral. The doctor shared with the other two that he was sure the man didn't intend for him to put the entire $10,000 in the casket. After all, he had given him medical attention whenever the man needed it. So what the doctor did was put in $7,000 and kept $3,000 for himself as a bonus.

The pastor then shared how much the man enjoyed the choir at church. It always made him smile. So, because the church was in need of a new organ which was going to cost around $2,000, the pastor put $8,000 in the casket and kept $2,000 out for the organ.

That's when the lawyer started talking. As you know, lawyers have a reputation for being shrewd. The lawyer proceeded to tell the men, "Well, I kept my $10,000. I also went to the coffin and took your $7,000 and your $8,000 out and kept it too. Then I wrote him a check for the full $30,000 and placed it in his coffin. That way he's got his money!"

The lawyer leveraged his opportunity for greatest gain (although I'm not holding it up as an example!). The point is that when you are able to *legitimately* create increase in the realm of God's kingdom resources so that you can more fully pursue the advancement of His kingdom purposes, you are to do it.

Jesus didn't share this story to tell you how to get rich on earth, though. He shared this parable to illustrate how to think strategically for your eternal future. When you leave this life and head into eternity, there will be an opportunity for a Welcoming Committee. The question is how many people are going to be at the pearly gate to welcome you because of the impact you made on their lives spiritually.

> *Jesus is calling you to strategically prioritize the spiritual over the material.*

Did you disciple, mentor, and guide others on how to have their sin debt paid in full through the death, burial, and resurrection of Jesus Christ? Did you show others how to profit spiritually on earth by overcoming Satan's schemes? Did you use your time, talents, and treasures shrewdly in order to help others experience a greater level of spiritual productivity themselves?

Jesus is calling you to strategically prioritize the spiritual over the material. He uses the material (money) to teach a point about the spiritual. As we read further in Luke 16, this distinction is clearly made. "No servant can serve two masters; for either he will hate the one and love the other, or else he will be devoted to one and despise the other. You cannot serve God and wealth" (verse 13).

By showing the tangible connection between the unrighteous steward's present with his future, Jesus is trying to help us make a mental connection between our present and our future as well. When a person fails to be strategic with their time, talents, and treasures on earth as a steward for God's kingdom purposes, that person will reach the time of accounting on Judgment Day and have nothing to show for it. Yes, salvation is free, based on faith alone in Christ alone. But rewards come tied to what you do on earth.

Influencing others in a way that brings God glory fulfills the greatest commandments we've been given, which are to love God with all of our hearts and to love others as we love ourselves.

You and I must learn to live on earth in light of this future reality. We must make our decisions with an eternal perspective in mind. As much as possible, you must attach the spiritual to every choice you make, word you say, and thought you think. In so doing, you are seeking to impact the lives of people for good.

Influencing others in a way that brings God glory fulfills the greatest commandments we've been given, which are to love God with all of our hearts and to love others as we love ourselves (Luke 10:27). Fulfilling these commandments means you and I are to be strategic about how we bring positive impact to others, in such a way that brings God glory.

By reducing the debt of those who owed money to the owner, the shrewd manager brought them good. He also made his owner look good because the debtors assumed this idea came from the owner himself. Not only was it a great business decision, it was also a tremendous PR move for the owner's reputation. When you and I seek to better the lives of all we come in contact with—whether in word or deed—we not only positively influence them but we also bring God the honor that is due Him.

The Good Works of Stewardship

But keep in mind that good things must always be tied to the spiritual if they are to have an eternal impact. Nice things and good things by themselves aren't good enough. Non-Christians do good things. You don't have to be a follower of Jesus Christ to be benevolent. You don't have to be a disciple to be a great neighbor, to feed the homeless, build a hospital, or help people improve their job situation. Those are all good things. But only when good things are tied to God's glory do they become the "good works" we are called to do as believers in Christ (Matthew 5:16). See, a good work is more than a good thing. A good work is when God is attached to it. It has the eternal wrapped into it. By bringing the gospel, discipleship, and the Word of God into the good things you invest in, you have brought the spiritual into the physical realm. You have turned a temporal thing into an eternal thing.

> *See, a good work is more than a good thing. A good work is when God is attached to it. It has the eternal wrapped into it.*

For example, let's say you are in a high-rise hotel and you are waiting for the elevator. When the elevator door opens, you realize that the elevator car is not there. It's just a big, empty hole dropping multiple floors to the ground. Somehow something went wrong and the elevator car didn't come up to your floor. Now, if you stepped through those open doors, disaster would swallow you up quickly. But, thankfully, you catch yourself and don't step into the giant chasm.

A few seconds after you realize the issue at hand, a blind man walks around the corner of the hotel elevator waiting area. The blind man is making his way to the exact same elevator you just saved yourself from stepping into. When you look down, you notice that the blind man's shoes are untied. Concerned that he may trip over his untied shoes, you stop him and ask him if you can tie his shoes for him. Of course he lets you do that because that is a very good thing for you to do. You just saved him from tripping.

But after you tie his shoes, he continues to walk toward the still-open door at the elevator. Yet even though the open door leads to a drop of multiple floors, you don't say anything. After all, you just did one good thing. No need to go overboard on this day. So, you just let him keep walking toward the door. And while he no longer has any risk of tripping over his untied shoes because of the good thing you did, he still falls to his death in the elevator shaft because you didn't impact his destiny. His destiny was disaster. Even though you delivered him from momentary issues, you did not inform him on how to be delivered from long-term issues—in this case, death itself.

Doing good things for people, when those good things do not involve their eternal destiny or eternal reward, is simply doing good things for people. Feeding the poor; helping the homeless; visiting the sick, incarcerated, or homebound—these are all good. It's just that when they are done apart from an eternal view and eternal connection, their impact is only in the here and now. Sure, the person may not trip over an untied shoelace, but that person will still walk steadily toward a destiny of disaster when you do not use your influence in doing good works that are connected to God. It takes both the good deed and the gospel in order to be considered a good work. Helping people recover from life's negative realities is a good and important thing to do. But if they die without Christ, they have been hit with a blow they can never recover from.

What Jesus seeks to teach each of us through this parable is that our eternal rewards are tied to how wisely we use the spiritual influence He has given to us on earth. We have been invested with the spiritual authority of the Owner to release people from bondage, to set the captives free, and to cancel debts that Satan has sought to destroy people's lives with. Jesus has given us the power to do even greater works than He did while on earth. John 14:12-14 says clearly, "Truly, truly, I say to you, he who believes in Me, the works that I do, he will do also; and greater works than these he will do; because I go to the Father. Whatever you ask in My name, that will I do, so that the Father may be glorified in the Son. If you ask Me anything in My name, I will do it."

> *We have been invested with the spiritual authority of the Owner to release people from bondage, to set the captives free, and to cancel debts that Satan has sought to destroy people's lives with.*

What are the works that Jesus did? Jesus speaks of Himself in Luke 7:22, "Go and report to John what you have seen and heard: the blind receive sight, the lame walk, the lepers are cleansed, and the deaf hear, the dead are raised up, the poor have the gospel preached to them." Yes, Jesus tied up the untied shoes. He did the good things to help people in the here and now. But He connected it to the spiritual. Look closely at how He closes out His statement about His works: "The poor have the gospel preached to them."

God wants you to do great and mighty works in His name in order to release people from the bonds of the creditor, the enemy himself. He's tasked you and me with this responsibility, and He's even given us His authority to do it. But, as Jesus said earlier in the parable, if you are not faithful with the use of unrighteous wealth, who is going to trust you with true riches? Before He gives you more, God wants to see what you are doing with what you have, because "he who is faithful in a very little thing is faithful also in much" (Luke 16:10). It's about being faithful (1 Corinthians 4:2), which means being consistently dependable over time.

True Riches

The faithful steward who strategically uses the spiritual access, authority, gifts, talents, and treasures God has given will experience the rewards of "true riches." Now, I don't want you to confuse "true riches" with "wealth." In fact, one can have true riches while still having very little money. Jesus made a clear distinction between the two in His statement on both. He said if someone is not faithful stewarding unrighteous "wealth," then who would trust that person with "true riches"? The reason these are different is because true riches have nothing to do with money. True riches are when God invades your circumstances and becomes so real to you that you can reach out and touch Him. True riches are when the spiritual leaves heaven and joins you on earth to affect your circumstances. True riches are when heaven shows you how much God has in His bank account even when all of your bank accounts have run dry.

True riches are when God invades your circumstances and becomes so real to you that you can reach out and touch Him.

True riches involve God's hand. His provision. The manifestation of His power. The intervention of God Himself.

Not too long ago I went to my doctor for a checkup and he asked me if he'd ever told me his story about encountering an angel. Now, I know that my doctor is a strong believer because I've gone to him for decades. He's a nationally renowned physician who openly uses his platform to promote God's glory. But in all of those years he had not told me about the angel. So I asked him to tell me what happened.

That's when Dr. Cooper shared with me about the time he was doing missional medical work in a communist country, and he ran into an issue with his passport. The problem with his passport was so severe that it would not have allowed him to return to the States at the end of his trip. In fact, he had been told that he would be locked up as the authorities in the communist country researched the issue. Dr. Cooper paused a moment as he told me this story. I could tell that even the thought of being locked up in that country so many years ago caused him fear. He admitted that he panicked when the person told him about this issue with his passport.

But then he did something very wise. He prayed. Dr. Cooper said, "Lord, please intervene in this because I cannot fix this. I don't know how to fix this, and I was even unaware of the issue to begin with. But now they are saying they can lock me up over it and I'm asking You to get me home somehow."

Dr. Cooper proceeded to the special security passport line to see what the authorities would tell him next. He was next in line with just a couple in front of him when he said that a lady dressed in white from head to toe came alongside of him. The lady said to him, "Excuse me, Doctor. I've been looking for you. Give me your passport."

Dr. Cooper shared how he had never seen this woman before. But something about her brought him comfort. So he handed her his passport. Then she told him to come with her up to the clerk's window. When they reached the window, she said to the man on the other side of the glass, "Stamp his passport." The man did so and said to the doctor, "Sir, here's your stamped passport." When Dr. Cooper turned to thank the lady for what she had done, she was nowhere to be found. So he just looked at the man and his stamped passport and proceeded to get on his flight to go home.

"Tony," he told me with a smile breaking out over his face, "she was an angel. I have no doubt about it."

That's true riches.

Dr. Cooper is, by the world's standards, a very successful man. He's the noted founder of the aerobics movement. Yet with all of his material assets, he could not have bought his way out of that situation. There was something wrong with his passport that only God could fix. True riches are greater than money. True riches tap into the power of God Himself.

> *Unless you are in touch with the spiritual, you don't have eyes to see or ears to hear true riches.*

As a pastor of a large congregation, I have often been invited to spend people's last moments with them. Witnessing the peace that comes on their faces as they recognize Jesus is near is nothing short of amazing. Not long ago we had a member of the church named Rosie who suffered from a terminal illness. As Rosie's time to go home drew nearer, God gave her a dream. In that dream, He told her that the very next day would be her last day and that she was to gather her children around her to say good-bye until they met again on the other side. The next afternoon, after saying good-bye to her family, she passed away.

That's true riches, when you get to see the supernatural invade the natural. But unless you are in touch with the spiritual, you don't have eyes to see or ears to hear true riches. Money can't buy you what you need most—supernatural guidance, peace, joy, contentment, hope, deliverance, spiritual insight, and an abundant eternal reward. These are the true riches God provides that should motivate us to willingly and joyfully pursue the privilege of kingdom generosity as His kingdom stewards. People can't give you those things. Power can't give you those things. Your 401(k) or mutual funds can't give you those things. True riches are accessed when you shrewdly and strategically invest your time, talents, and treasures into the things of God. As kingdom stewards, God is asking each of us to use every opportunity to do good in order to create an eternal impact. God will not give true riches to bad stewards.

If you will strategize the spiritual and bring that strategy into all things that you do in the material world, you will store up for yourself true riches. These riches will benefit you in both time and eternity.

Use what God has given you. Use the authority He's provided you in His name. Set people free from bondage through discipling them, helping the poor and oppressed, and pointing them to the Savior. As you cut the cords of Satan's hold on others, you are laying up for yourself treasures that no moth will eat and no rust will destroy. You are also allowing your finances to shape your heart Godward instead of allowing money (or the things it can buy) to become an idol in your life, thus taking you further from God (Matthew 6:19-21). By investing in others' spiritual growth shrewdly, strategically, and proactively, you are—for all intents and purposes—according to Jesus, investing in yourself. You are stealing the ball from the enemy and scoring in your own basket. Remember, you can use money to serve God (Biblical Prosperity), but you must never seek to use God to serve money (Prosperity Theology).

You can use money to serve God (Biblical Prosperity), but you must never seek to use God to serve money (Prosperity Theology).

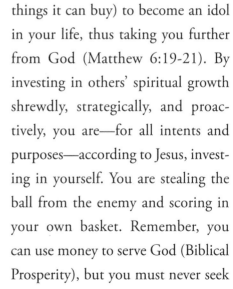

No basketball coach would be satisfied if his team opted for sitting on the bench and watching the game. Neither would he be satisfied if a player did like Jonathan did and scored in the opposing team's basket. Basketball requires an intentional strategy—effort, diligence, and direction. Similarly, Jesus has reminded us through this story that strategically stewarding our time, talents, and treasures for the benefit of others and the glory of God is what you and I ought to be about. By becoming a strategic kingdom steward, you can change the trajectory of your life on earth and receive greater reward in heaven. That's our game plan. That's our approach. No more standing on the sidelines or sitting on the bench. No more scoring for the enemy. God has equipped and called His stewards to strategically advance His kingdom. To do anything less is doing layups for the enemy.

PART III

THE
APPROACH
OF
KINGDOM
STEWARDSHIP

7

PRIMACY

Did you know there are certain things God cannot do? Now, before you close this book and start writing me an email with words like "heresy" in it, let me explain myself. I understand that the common thought is that God can do everything. But that's not entirely true. There exist some things God simply cannot do.

For example, God cannot lie. God exists as truth, embodies truth, and can speak only truth. Lying sits outside of His ability and nature (Hebrews 6:18). God cannot contradict His core character.

Another thing God cannot do is stop being God. He is the same in His essential Being and attributes yesterday, today, and forever (Hebrews 13:8). He also cannot sin or cause us to sin (James 1:13), due to the purity of His own makeup. Holiness and sinfulness cannot abide together, thus God cannot provoke sin in His own children within whom He resides.

See, there are a number of things God cannot do. One more thing He cannot do is He can't be second. God must be first. Always first. Never second, and certainly not less than that either. Yet unfortunately today we live in a world where most people, particularly in western culture, acknowledge God but do not give Him the position He deserves. They do not make Him first. First in their thoughts. First in their hearts. First in their priorities. First in their choices. First.

If you'll do a search of Scripture, it won't take you long to find places where God is demanding to be put first. In fact, the word "first" pops up a lot in the Bible—in relationship to God. For an example of this, see Matthew 6:33. God literally audits His position in people's lives. He won't take your word for it. Just because someone says God is first in his or her life doesn't mean God believes it. He audits each of us to see if He truly does hold the placement of first over all else.

In baseball, there are certain requirements that must take place in order for a team to score a run. One of the most basic requirements involves touching each base. When a player runs to first base, he must touch first base. In fact, if he skips first base, then the other bases he touches become irrelevant. Even if he crosses home plate, he will still be called "out" by the umpire if he failed to touch first base.

> *Treat God like He's second fiddle in your life and you'll reap the consequences.*

A lot of people want God to empower them to hit home runs in their lives, all the while skipping first base. But God cannot be second. You cannot skip God and expect to win in life. Whatever you pursue must come after God. Not before. And definitely not instead of Him.

Remember, kingdom stewards are believers who faithfully oversee the protection and expansion of the assets God has entrusted to them to manage on His behalf. A steward is a manager, not an owner. The moment you think you are an owner and start acting like an owner by making up your own rules, you are in conflict with the real Owner. Treat God like He's second fiddle in your life and you'll reap the consequences.

It always amazes me how we can understand and apply the principle of priorities to people in our lives but not so easily to the God of the universe. Let me give you a personal example to illustrate this. I have a very busy schedule. My speaking, meeting, studying, and counseling schedule is typically planned out a year in advance. Dates are locked and calendars are finalized. However, not too long ago I got a phone call from former President George W. Bush. He called me personally to invite himself to lunch.

You better believe I cancelled things on my already full schedule and made room for the former president to come to the church and have lunch with me on the following Tuesday. Now, Tuesdays are my busiest days of my very busy weeks. But the former president indicated that he wanted to come on a Tuesday. So, Tuesday with the president it was. I made room. Why? Because when a former president of the United States invites himself over for lunch, you make room. His position demands priority.

God knows we do that for people. God sees us clear our calendars and direct our attention to people whom we prioritize. He sees this take place all the time. We'll even devote more time to things like social media (scrolling through posts from perfect strangers half the time) rather than spending time with God—the God who gives us breath, eyes to see, and a mind to think.

You can bet that God does not take this sitting down. God is love, yes. God loved each of us enough to send His Son as a sacrifice on our behalf. But that does not mean God is a pushover. In Malachi 1:6-9, we hear His words as He condemns the Israelite priests for giving him secondhand worship. We read,

> "'A son honors his father, and a servant his master. Then if I am a father, where is My honor? And if I am a master, where is My respect?' says the LORD of hosts to you, O priests who despise My name. But you say, 'How have we despised Your name?' You are presenting defiled food upon My altar. But you say, 'How have we defiled You?' In that you say, 'The table of the LORD is to be despised.' But when you present the blind for sacrifice, is it not evil? And when you present the lame and sick, is it not evil? Why

not offer it to your governor? Would he be pleased with you? Or would he receive you kindly?" says the LORD of hosts. "But now will you not entreat God's favor, that He may be gracious to us? With such an offering on your part, will He receive any of you kindly?" says the LORD of hosts.

God calls the priests on the carpet. He doesn't mince His words. He asks them point-blank, "Would you give these sacrifices to your governor?" It's a rhetorical question because the answer is an obvious "No." And yet the priests somehow thought it was okay to treat God with less respect than their politicians. Anything less than our best is an insult to the Owner and Creator of all. He is our great King (Malachi 1:14). We have no excuse for giving God our leftovers.

> *Anything less than our best is an insult to the Owner and Creator of all. He is our great King.*

Suppose you went to a restaurant, placed your order, and the waiter brought you leftovers. What if you saw him scraping off other people's plates onto yours? What would you do when he handed you a plate full of leftovers? You, like me, would get up and leave that restaurant right then and there. Even if the waiter urged you to eat because the other people seemed to enjoy it, you wouldn't partake. No, you would leave. And rightfully so. The reason you would not accept it is because of the price they said you would have to pay for it. No one is paying for leftovers.

Friend, God paid a high price to be first place in your life.

He doesn't want your leftovers.

He doesn't deserve your leftovers.

In Haggai 1, we get a glimpse into His heart again as He rebukes His followers for their selfish focus on their own pleasures and status, all the while neglecting Him. Haggai may not be a popular book for devotions because it holds within it some tough truths. But if you and I neglect to apply the principles located in this book to our daily stewardship choices, we will experience the results that the people in this passage experienced. God's precepts remain unchanged. We read in Haggai 1:1-11,

> In the second year of Darius the king, on the first day of the sixth month, the word of the Lord came by the prophet Haggai to Zerubbabel the son of Shealtiel, governor of Judah, and to Joshua the son of Jehozadak, the high priest, saying, "Thus says the Lord of hosts, 'This people says, "The time has not come, even the time for the house of the Lord to be rebuilt."'" Then the word of the Lord came by Haggai the prophet, saying, "Is it time for you yourselves to dwell in your paneled houses while this house lies desolate?" Now therefore, thus says the Lord of hosts, "Consider your ways! You have sown much, but harvest little; you eat, but there is not enough to be satisfied; you drink, but there is not enough to become drunk; you put on clothing, but no one is warm enough; and he who earns, earns wages to put into a purse with holes."
>
> Thus says the Lord of hosts, "Consider your ways! Go up to the mountains, bring wood and rebuild the temple, that I may be pleased with it and be glorified," says the Lord. "You look for much, but behold, it comes to little; when you bring it home, I blow it away. Why?" declares the Lord of hosts, "Because of My house which lies desolate, while each of you runs to his own house. Therefore, because of you the sky has withheld its dew and the earth has withheld its produce. I called for a drought on the land, on the mountains, on the grain, on the new wine, on the oil, on what the ground produces, on men, on cattle, and on all the labor of your hands."

The people this passage was addressed to had focused heavily on building their own homes and establishing their own comfort levels, all the while neglecting the building of God's temple. As a result, they suffered loss when God chose to withhold the provision from them, which was His to supply. God will get the respect due Him, one way or the other. You and I are given the opportunity to show honor willingly, or through the consequences our choices bring about.

Putting God First in Our Lives

The priority of a kingdom steward must always be God the King.

Most people, even Christians, have God in the kitchen of their lives, and not in the den. If a family puts a television in the kitchen, it is there to be glanced at. People don't typically sit on a stool and watch entire movies from start to finish in the kitchen. The television in the kitchen exists to provide updates here or there from shows such as the news, game shows, or cooking shows. It is there so that while someone is cooking or cleaning, they can hear or see a bit of entertainment and information.

> *If you relegate God to anything less than first, you have removed Him from the primacy of active involvement in your life.*

But the television in the den is for the full experience. That's where people sit in their easy chairs, grab a blanket, and watch an entire game or movie. In fact, you'll never find a big screen TV in the kitchen. But you will find one in the den because that's where you can focus.

Far too many believers keep God in the kitchen of their lives. He is there, sure. You might glance at a verse or think about a passage while you do other things in your life. But He is not the priority. He doesn't get your undivided attention. But like I said earlier, God doesn't go for that. He cannot be second, third, or anywhere else in your priorities but first. God is to be the sun of your solar system, where the activities of your life revolve around Him and Him alone. If you relegate God to anything less than first, you have removed Him from the primacy of active involvement in your life.

Know that truth. Embrace that truth. That truth impacts you far more than you may even realize. The further you move God down the line of your priorities, the less involved He is in your life. The less power of the Spirit you tap into, the less consistency of favor and grace you activate. The less peace and calm He supplies. Not because it isn't there to supply but because you have chosen not to prioritize Him in your life.

When you have to choose between His will and your own, you choose His. God says if He is not at that level of love in your life, then you are not worthy of Him.

God wants and deserves to be first in all areas of our lives. But there are a number of areas He keys in on for us to examine in Scripture. For starters, God wants to be first in your affections. Revelation 2:4 says, "But I have this against you, that you have left your first love," in spite of the fact that these believers were commended for their orthodoxy and religious activity. But it was not enough when first love was missing. He doesn't chastise them for not loving Him at all. The love is still there. It's just no longer first.

In Matthew 10:37-38, He explains first love this way, "He who loves father or mother more than Me is not worthy of Me; and he who loves son or daughter more than Me is not worthy of Me. And he who does not take his cross and follow after Me is not worthy of Me." God wants you to love Him more than you even love your family. Beyond that, He emphasizes in verse 38 that He wants you to love Him more than you even love yourself. To deny yourself and take up your cross means to put His desires, His goals, and His priorities above your own. When you have to choose between His will and your own, you choose His. God says if He is not at that level of love in your life, then you are not worthy of Him. It's plain and simple. God doesn't mince words. He doesn't stutter. If He's not first in your priorities, then you don't deserve His involvement in your life and our stewardship becomes greatly impeded.

Now, these verses were written to disciples. Eternal salvation is secure through faith alone in Christ alone. But marginalizing God in your life removes His active engagement with you. God demands to be first in your affections. He wants to be your primary love relationship. He wants your greatest pursuit to be that of pursuing intimacy with Him. He demands to be first in your devotion. Suppose your mate says to you, "I will fulfill my duties in this marriage, but you won't be first in my life." Such an attitude would remove the value of even good actions. Duty, in a marriage, is never to be disconnected from devotion. Similarly, neither is devotion to be disconnected from a kingdom steward's relationship with God. Loving God first is the most important step in getting everything else (including your finances) into proper working order (Matthew 6:33; Revelation 2:1-7).

But not only does He want to be first in your affections, He also wants to be first in your worship. In the Old Testament culture, they worshiped on Saturday. The New Testament culture shifted worship to Sunday. Sunday was, and is, the first day of the week. Not only that, but the prioritization of giving (which is a form of worship that we will look at more deeply a little later in this chapter) was also moved to the first day of the week. This way, the people honored God with the firstfruits before all the other expenses got paid. We read about this prioritization in 1 Corinthians 16:2: "On the first day of every week each one of you is to put aside and save, as he may prosper, so that no collections be made when I come."

In fact, the Resurrection happened on the first day of the week and this designation of worship was to celebrate and commemorate the risen Savior. Colossians 1:15-18 speaks to the "firstness" of Christ. It says,

> He is the image of the invisible God, the firstborn of all creation. For by Him all things were created, both in the heavens and on earth, visible and invisible, whether thrones or dominions or rulers or authorities—all things have been created through Him and for Him. He is before all things, and in Him all things hold together. He is also head of the body, the church; and He is the beginning, the firstborn from the dead, so that He Himself will come to have first place in everything.

For Jesus to hold the position of "first place in everything" means there cannot be any category of your life where He does not dominate. When we break down the meaning of the word "everything," we discover that it means "every" thing. That may have been obvious to you, yet far too many of us miss it. Jesus made everything and so He owns everything. As a result, He rules everything as well. If you are going to truly be a kingdom steward, His viewpoint dictates your viewpoint. His will informs your will. Everything in your life must surrender to your commitment to Jesus and His say-so in your thoughts, words, and decisions.

Everything in your life must surrender to your commitment to Jesus and His say-so in your thoughts, words, and decisions.

In addition to being first in our affections and in our worship, God wants us to always pray to Him first. We read in 1 Timothy 2:1, "First of all, then, I urge that entreaties and prayers, petitions and thanksgivings, be made on behalf of all men." Notice how he starts out the call to prayer with the word "first." We are to start with prayer. God doesn't call us to pray after we have made a mess. He didn't establish prayer as an avenue of communication with Him for only those times when we need help out of a crisis. God wants us to pray first. Talk to Him first. Consult Him first.

> *God's Word holds the answers to every question. But you will never locate that answer if you don't go to Him first—through your affection, worship, prayer, and study of His Word.*

And not only are we to consult Him in prayer but we are also to consult Him through His Word. We are to first see what God has to say on the subject and not what humanity believes (Romans 3:4). God's Word holds the answers to every question. But you will never locate that answer if you don't go to Him first—through your affection, worship, prayer, and study of His Word.

That's what's wrong with so many Christians today. God's not first. He's in the mix somewhere. He's in consideration, sure. But He's not the first point of consultation and communication. He's not the first point of trust, affection, communion, and worship. He's just in there somewhere. Yet God says that "somewhere" is unacceptable simply because of who He is. He is God. He is the Creator. He is the Owner. He is first.

Giving to God First

Now, don't read that subhead "Giving to God First" and then skip to the next chapter. Most people struggle with this next area we are going to look at. I understand. But as you will see, when you rob God, you rob yourself. Giving is an issue of honor. Many want to use God for emergencies rather than to honor Him for who He is and for what He has already done. Reading, learning, and applying the spiritual principles of tithing and giving will open the storehouses of God's provision in your life. As Proverbs 3:9-10 shows us, there is a return on your investment when you give to God. "Honor the LORD from your wealth and from the first of all your produce; so your barns will be filled with plenty and your vats will overflow with new wine."

Giving to God first reveals the level at which you honor Him in your heart.

We looked at the garden in the first section of this book but I want to revisit it here in the context of giving. When God established the Garden of Eden, He created it as a homestead for Adam and Eve. The garden was their house. In the middle of their house, God put a tree. He called it the tree of the knowledge of good and evil. It was a Google tree, an information center. Multitudes of trees existed elsewhere throughout the garden from which Adam and Eve could freely eat. But the tree that stood in the middle of their house—that was off-limits. God

Giving to God first reveals the level at which you honor Him in your heart.

clearly instructed them not to mess with that tree. God did not want them gaining information and determining right from wrong, apart from Him.

Why do you think God put that tree smack dab in the middle of their house? Because Adam and Eve would have to pass it wherever they went. This is similar to when I was in seminary and Lois and I were house-sitting. We had to walk by the car, house, pool, and all the furnishings all the while knowing it was not ours. We were simply using it, not owning it. Only the owner makes the rules.

Adam and Eve had to walk by the tree as well. When they went to their bedroom, they would pass it. When they went to the kitchen, they would pass it. When they went to take a walk, they would pass it. God placed it there as a perpetual reminder that, although they lived in this house, He owned it. The Garden of Eden was His. He was just letting them stay there in order to fulfill His kingdom purpose as His stewards.

The Garden of Eden isn't the only time God sought to make this point to His people. The tithe was established as a tangible way of demonstrating recognition of God as the owner and source of all. In Deuteronomy 14:23, God tells us that the tithe is a lesson. It's a spiritual lesson enacted by God through which we are to learn to fear Him. His words, not mine. We read, "You shall eat in the presence of the LORD your God, at the place where He chooses to establish His name, the tithe of your grain, your new wine, your oil, and the firstborn of your herd and your flock, so that you may learn to fear the LORD your God always." As we have seen elsewhere, to "fear" God is to take Him seriously.

The tithe tangibly demonstrates that you believe God is your Source. *Saying* that God is your Source means nothing. Words alone mean nothing. God doesn't believe you just because you say something. God believes you when He sees that your actions back your words. Tithing is an act of faith. Especially when it's given first—before your bills are paid or your entertainment choices are made. The entirety of Deuteronomy 26 talks about the importance of giving to God first.

A lot of Christians don't understand the connection between the spiritual and the economic. Leviticus 26:14-39, among many other places in Scripture, makes this connection for us. In this passage God spells out direct correlations between the Israelites rebelling against honoring Him first and the results of that rebellion. I won't include all twenty-six verses here but I encourage you to read them on your own. The results for failing to honor God through obedience to His commands, including the command of giving to Him the firstfruits, are:

- sudden terrors
- fevers and disease

- sowing seed for the enemies to consume
- oppression
- fear and anxiety
- fruitlessness of the land and trees
- and much more!

Loss, worry, destruction, and disaster await those who rebel against God's spiritual principles. In other words, the spiritual must come before the economic. Many of our economic problems are related to our spiritual condition.

God is not asking for a donation when He asks His stewards to give to Him. We get it all mixed up when we think that way. You and I are not donating to God when we give to our church or other ministries. God owns it already. He owns what we have already. It's His. In fact, Malachi goes so far as to say that we are robbing God when we don't give to Him. Malachi 3:8-9 says, "Will a man rob God? Yet you are robbing Me! But you say, 'How have we robbed You?' In tithes and offerings. You are cursed with a curse, for you are robbing Me, the whole nation of you!"

You and I are not donating to God when we give to our church or other ministries. God owns it already.

I'm fairly certain when a robber considers a potential target, he or she doesn't choose the police station. That's not a good idea. Neither is robbing the Source of all things—God Himself—a bright idea either. But that's what we do when we withhold the honor He is rightfully due. We've got all of these Christians in our nation today, and around the world, who are wanting God to unlock the windows of heaven in order to pour down blessings and favor, all the while stealing from Him! That's not how it works. God tells us how it works when we read in Malachi 3:10-12:

"Bring the whole tithe into the storehouse, so that there may be food in My house, and test Me now in this," says the LORD of hosts, "if I will not open for you the windows of heaven and pour out for you a blessing until it overflows. Then I will rebuke the devourer for you, so that it will not destroy the fruits of the ground; nor will your vine in the field cast its grapes," says the LORD of hosts. "All the nations will call you blessed, for you shall be a delightful land," says the LORD of hosts.

God stands behind His Word. He knows that what He is saying is true. In fact, God challenges us to "test Him" in what He says in this very passage. Unfortunately, a lot of us are not receiving all that God legitimately has in store for us because we won't even "test Him." Yet God has declared that He won't give to a thief. When you rob God of what is rightfully His—first place in the treasures He's given you to steward—you cannot simultaneously ask Him to give you more. When you rob God, you are really robbing yourself. God wants you to trust Him. He wants you to believe Him. He wants you to act in faith. So, He gives you an opportunity to do all of that through tithes and offerings.

> *When you rob God of what is rightfully His—first place in the treasures He's given you to steward—you cannot simultaneously ask Him to give you more.*

A Priest Named Melchizedek

The framework for our giving shows up early in Scripture. In Genesis 14:17-20, we read that Abram is coming back from a battle in which

God had given him the victory. As he heads back from war, he runs into a priest named Melchizedek. The interesting thing about this priest is that he is also a king. Melchizedek brings bread and wine to Abram in celebration of the victory. With the bread and wine, he also gave Abram his blessing. Then, after the communion together and blessing, Abram gave Melchizedek a tenth (a tithe) of what he had gotten in the battle.

Immediately after this, another king—the king of Sodom—tried to trick Abram. He tried to manipulate Abram in such a way that would make it look as if Sodom was the true benefactor of Abram's wealth. But because Abram had spent time in communion with Melchizedek and had received the blessing of spiritual guidance and refreshment, he didn't fall for the king of Sodom's trick. He had just come from one battle and he was about to head into another battle of a different kind with the king of Sodom, a battle of the mind and of words. But in between the first battle and the second battle, Abram experienced communion, refreshment, and the opportunity to honor God with what he had.

The lesson for us today in our contemporary culture runs deep in this biblical account. The book of Hebrews emphasizes that Jesus is the great High Priest, after the order of Melchizedek (Hebrews 5:6; 6:20; 7:17). Within that role, He intercedes for us (Hebrews 7:25), similar to how Melchizedek interceded in Abram's life and brought him refreshment. Jesus' role, while seated at the right hand of the Father, is to intercede for you and me. His job is to intercede in our circumstances. It is His responsibility to place Himself in the middle of our circumstances.

Melchizedek met Abram as he came out of one victory and was about to head into another battle. That second battle turned into a victory as well because Abram had the opportunity to be refreshed in between. In essence, his priest and king had him covered on both sides. I wonder if anyone reading these pages needs to be covered by Jesus on both sides of the battle.

The same refreshment, communion, and blessing Abram had with Melchizedek is available to each of us today through our great High

Priest, Jesus Christ. But just as important—the same tithe Abram gave to Melchizedek is ours to give to Jesus as well. In fact, Hebrews 7:8 recognizes the transition of the giving of tithes to Jesus in the new covenant age when it says, "In this case mortal men receive tithes, but in that case one receives them, of whom it is witnessed that he lives on." In the new covenant, giving tithes and offerings reflects honor and trust. Abram gave out of gratitude, not compulsion. Likewise, we are to give to God what is God's out of gratitude to Him.

I often hear of some confusion when people talk about tithes and offerings. The tithe is what we have been instructed to give, which is 10 percent. The tithe establishes our recognition of God as our sovereign Source (Deuteronomy 14:23). The offering is over and above the tithe. In Scripture, this is often referred to as a freewill offering. This is a voluntary gift given over and above the tithe to express our love, appreciation, and gratitude for God's goodness to us (Deuteronomy 16:10; Ezra 3:5). Until you have given the tithe, you haven't given an offering.

In 1 Chronicles, we see an example of this offering motivated by gratitude and worship when King David and the Israelites gave in abundance of what they had in order that the temple of God would be completely filled with all it needed. We read in 1 Chronicles 29:9, "Then the people rejoiced because they had offered so willingly, for they made their offering to the LORD with a whole heart, and King David also rejoiced greatly." While the tithe belongs to the

Giving is an act of worship.

local church that feeds you God's Word and ministers to the flock and the community (the storehouse), the offering should be given as the Holy Spirit moves upon the heart of the giver regarding a specific ministry, impact, or opportunity.

Whether it is the tithe or the offering, God is honored when we recognize His ownership over all we have. Giving is an act of worship and reflects our view of God. It is not to be given just to fulfill a religious obligation (i.e., legalism) but rather to express our trust in and need for and gratitude to our great God, who is the Source of all we possess. Remember, God loves a cheerful giver (2 Corinthians 9:6-7). When Cain and Abel came to worship God, the Bible says that Cain's offering of fruits and vegetables was rejected by God. While no direct reason why Cain's offering wasn't accepted is given in the Scripture, there is a direct reason why Abel's was. His brother Abel's offering was accepted because he had given the best of the best—the firstlings of his flock (Genesis 4:4).

God is worthy of being given the best of the best, and being given it first. We do this when we put Him first in our affections, first in our consideration, first in our consultation, first in our worship, first in our tithes, and first in our offerings. When He sees that you honor Him with your time, talents, and treasures, He responds to that honor graciously. Psalm 50:14-15 says, "Offer to God a sacrifice of thanksgiving and pay your vows to the Most High; call upon Me in the day of trouble; I shall rescue you, and you will honor Me."

Be stingy with God and He will be stingy with you (Proverbs 11:24). If you want to see and experience more of God's intervention, favor, and provision in your life, then put Him first. Don't pray to Him last. Pray to Him first. Don't go to His Word last. Go to His Word first. Don't love Him last. Love Him first. Kingdom stewardship demands the prioritization of God in all things.

More of us need to realize that God is not some robot sitting off in never-never land. We are made in His image. We have emotions. You can rest assured that God has emotions too. God feels. He gets angry. He becomes glad. He gets jealous. He desires your love and your worship. And not just the words of your love. He craves the actions of your love. He wants to know He is first. One way we demonstrate this is through tithes and offerings.

While preaching a sermon on this subject, I wanted to really bring this point home so I brought out nine red apples and one green apple. I also had our worship team place a large standing cross on the stage near the pulpit. To illustrate the principle of giving a tithe, I placed all nine red apples on the pulpit one by one. Then I shared how God created these apples, provided these apples, and freely gave us these apples to enjoy any way we want. But the green apple (one tenth) is to be given back to Him as the tithe. At that point, I walked the green apple over to the cross and put it on the cross.

But then I paused. I grabbed the green apple and took a bite out of it and said, "Even though this apple belongs to God, we look at it and start chewing. We think about that vacation we'd like to take. Or that car we want to drive. Or those new clothes we'd like to have." With each statement, I ate more and more of that green apple until I was not only full, but there was only a core left.

Tossing that core to the bottom of the cross, I reminded the congregation that this is exactly what many of us do to God. We give Him the leftovers after we've not only enjoyed the nine, but have also eaten up the tenth. And somehow, someway we still expect Him to be happy we gave Him the core.

We do that with our money. But we also do that with our love. We do that with our worship. We do that with our prayers. We do that with our attention. We do that with our time, talents, and treasures. We toss God our leftovers and expect Him to applaud with gratitude, while also pouring down more and more blessings upon us.

That doesn't sound like the God of the Bible I've studied my whole life. And as you study more and more of His Word, you'll discover that's just not how God operates at all. He deserves our best. He demands our best. He cannot be second.

God must be first. When He is not the priority in your time, talents, and treasures, you are not only robbing God, you are also simultaneously robbing yourself.

A story is told of a man who robbed a bank in Ottawa, Canada, using a 1918 44-caliber Colt 45 revolver. Using that gun, he walked out of the bank with $6,000. What the robber didn't know was that the gun he used to rob the bank was worth $100,000 on its own. Essentially, he took a $100,000 revolver into a bank to get a $6,000 gain. When he later got arrested, he not only lost the $6,000 he had stolen but also the $100,000 he had rightfully owned.

What a lot of Christians don't understand is similar to what this robber didn't understand. They don't understand what they already hold in their hands.

If you truly knew who God is and all the spiritual blessings He has prepared for you, you wouldn't rob God. You wouldn't cheat God. You wouldn't marginalize God. He owns the cattle on a thousand hills. If you only knew where the true Source is of every single thing you will ever have, you would put Him first. You would honor Him. He is Your provider—not just of money but also of peace, stability, significance, contentment, joy, victory, and so much more. The bottom line for kingdom stewards is summarized in Jesus' words to seek first the kingdom of God and His righteousness and all these things will be added to you (Matthew 6:33). Therefore, spiritual development must precede and take priority over economic development.

> *If you only knew where the true Source is of every single thing you will ever have, you would put Him first. You would honor Him. He is Your provider— not just of money but also of peace, stability, significance, content- ment, joy, victory, and so much more.*

As kingdom stewards, we ought to never focus on anything longer or more intently than on God Himself. Knowing His heart. His words. His will. His perspective. His agenda. His presence. Knowing Him ought to be our highest priority. God deserves first place in our time, talents, and most certainly in our treasures. Remember, God never accepts being second.

8

PERSPECTIVE

The story is told about a man who had great concerns about a friend of his known to be a drunkard. His friend drank to the point of intoxication virtually every day. This pattern of consumption caused this man to worry over his friend's health and well-being. He considered what he could do to save his friend's life from the inevitable spiral of destruction it was in. That's when he came up with an idea.

The man decided to go to the local bar and spend some time with his friend. He went with the intention of giving him the right perspective on his alcoholism. When he found his friend at the bar, he asked the bartender to give him two glasses. One he was to fill with water and the other with booze. The bartender did as he was asked.

Then the friend took out a little package he had in his pocket, which held two worms. He put one worm in the glass with water first and showed his friend how the worm just swam around. Next he put the other worm in the glass with the alcohol and after only a few seconds, that worm died.

"Did you see that?" the man asked. "The worm died from the alcohol."

"Yes, I saw that," the friend replied.

"Did you get the point?" the man probed more deeply.

"I think I did," said the friend.

"Well, just to make sure you did," the man continued, "tell me what the point is."

The friend sighed, smiled, and turned to the man seeking to help him. "Well, I think the point is if you drink a lot of booze, you won't have worms!"

Obviously this man's friend did not get the point. The way he interpreted the lesson given to him had been filtered through his own lens, and so he lost out on the wisdom that could have eventually saved his life.

When it comes to this subject of kingdom stewardship, far too many believers do not get the point either. As a refresher, kingdom stewardship can be defined as the divinely authorized responsibility for believers to faithfully oversee the protection and expansion of the assets that God has entrusted to them to manage on His behalf. God has loaned each of us a certain amount of time, talents, and treasures to manage. But when we decide that we are the owners of these things and begin acting like we are the owners of these things, we have missed the point.

Stewardship is the management of that which belongs to another owner. If you deposit money in a bank, you want that bank to manage your money and not to act like they own your money. In fact, if a bank starts making illegitimate and unlawful decisions like they own the money they have been given to manage, they will be taken to court for fraud and theft. God doesn't take us to court for theft when we act as owners over what He's given us to manage. But we do lose out on the multiplicity of rewards, blessings, and continued favor that come from living wisely as a kingdom steward.

The story of the man and his friend in the bar is a made-up illustration designed to convey a point. But the story of another man, Paul, and his friend Timothy as recorded for us in 1 Timothy 6:6-10 is true, and it provides the biblical basis for each of us to live with a right perspective on stewardship. Paul lays out his fundamental principle in verse 6. This verse serves as a great insight into the perspective we are to have as a kingdom steward. It says, "But godliness actually is a means of great gain when accompanied by contentment."

So much wisdom is packed in this one statement. Friend, if you want to truly live a rich life, you must learn how to mix godliness with contentment. Paul gives us a process for achieving great gains in our life and that formula is: **godliness + contentment = great gain**. Combining these two things increases results—otherwise known as "great gain." Keep in mind, great gain here does not mean great material gain. It is referring to what I mentioned earlier as "true riches." Yes, that might include money but it also might not mean money.

Godliness is simply a lifestyle in which one seeks to please God. To live a godly life involves consistently reflecting the character of God in all that you do and say. It means remaining in the midst of God's presence. Now, a person can embody godliness but not achieve great gain when godliness is not coupled with contentment. When the motivation and parameters focus only on rules, rules, rules—all the while failing to include the essential element of contentment—a person can actually become paralyzed in their growth. This can quickly morph into pharisaical limitations constrained by pride, doubt, and endless effort. Godliness must be married to contentment if it is to produce great gain.

Knowing the opposite of something can often help us better understand what it is. The opposite of godliness is ungodliness. The opposite of contentment is discontentment. When we reverse the statement Paul made in this passage, we discover that ungodliness combined with discontentment results in great loss. This loss is the loss of "true riches" God

> *Friend, if you want to truly live a rich life, you must learn how to mix godliness with contentment.*

supplies. True riches show up in a variety of ways, not just monetarily. These riches, however, always allow us to experience God's reality in our lives and circumstances.

Thus, the amount of true riches you gain or lose in life is largely up to you. Are you seeking to live a life that honors the presence and rule of the Lord Jesus Christ each day, or are you seeking to please yourself according to the world's system of values? How you answer that question will have a direct impact on both the quality and legacy of your life.

Contentment

It's true that maintaining a heart of contentment can be a challenge in a culture comprised primarily of discontentment. We are reminded every day to be dissatisfied with our lot in life. Madison Avenue urges this dissatisfaction in us. They tell us that if we don't have the newest and the best, then we have to strive to get it so that we can be happy. Beyond Madison Avenue, our phones remind us to live with discontentment. As soon as a person gets the latest version of a smartphone, the company comes out with a new "latest" version of the smartphone. It's a continual cycle of obtaining something only to find out that there is something else better and more valuable to obtain all over again. Never mind that the previous version of smartphones still work. Functioning is not the criteria for smartphones, apparently. So the majority of smartphone users spend hundreds of dollars, if not even over a thousand dollars, every year or two to upgrade to the latest and greatest model. Keeping up with the Joneses has a brand-new meaning in the world in which we live today.

Social media is a constant source of discontentment for so many people. People browse, swipe, like, comment on, or scan other people's posts—and often these posts are written by strangers. This produces a comparison-trap mentality within many viewers. Seeing what they perceive to be prettier, wealthier, happier, or more polished versions of life and success only fuels the fire of low self-esteem and anxiety in countless minds and thoughts.

Satan has done a number on us in stoking the embers of discontentment. The reason why this area is such a great focus for him is because he knows the truth of Paul's words: Godliness plus contentment equals great gain. Religion alone won't produce great gain. Going to church and having your daily devotional time won't produce great gain. As long as Satan can keep you trapped in a spirit of want, lack, loss, or even envy and jealousy, he can keep you from God's gifts of great gain.

Satan has done a number on us in stoking the embers of discontentment.

Contentment means to be at ease on the inside, regardless of circumstances on the outside. It has to do with an inner trust and dependence upon God as we rest peacefully and thankfully in our present circumstances. It means to be okay where I am until I get to where I want to go. That clarification is critical because too many people assume that contentment means to give up the desire to go any further in life or experience a change in status of relationships, finances, or employment. To let all of your desires go reduces the spirit and soul to a mere robotic presence. We have been created in the image of God and as such have within us both the ability and desire to create, expand, and grow.

Contentment does not mean you shut down your emotions and settle for what you have. Contentment is not resignation to your lot in life. What contentment entails is while waiting and pursuing to do better, go further, or maximize your time, talents, and resources more completely, you are also entirely okay with where you are now. At the core of contentment is how you are rooted and grounded spiritually in the inner man. Not how things are happening for you externally.

The world operates by its unseen resources. For example, when you see a piece of fruit, the only way that fruit became fruit was due to the roots of the tree upon which the fruit grew. There exists something unseen that provides the way for the seen (the fruit) to come about. Likewise, when you witness a river flowing through the valley of a mountainous region, that river exists due to a number of unseen things such as the flow of the rains, the melting of snow from the mountaintops, and the provision of underground springs. Or similarly, the minerals that reside in the ground unseen provide for us the cars that we do see. These unseen resources give the visible benefit of the things we value.

> *Godliness with contentment provides stability on the inside regardless of circumstances on the outside.*

When a person combines biblical contentment with godliness, God then enables the roots to run deeper, the rains to pour more fully, and the minerals of His ministry to the saints to be tapped into. God allows you greater access into the provision of His unseen resources so that what becomes visible to yourself and others is great gain. Whether the great gain is emotional stability, wisdom, self-restraint, joy, faith, or anything else varies, based on the focus of your contentment. But whatever they are, they will produce visible fruit in your life. Godliness with contentment provides stability on the inside regardless of circumstances on the outside.

Not long ago I had the opportunity to tour both a ship and a submarine in the Baltimore Harbor. Both ships had been built to withstand the waves and weather found on the open seas. But the submarine was constructed in such a way as to have its inhabitants not even feel those effects. That is because when a submarine goes deep into the ocean, the external weather no longer rocks or tosses the boat around. The depth of the submarine doesn't change the weather. The weather could still be raging as a storm up above the surface of the sea. But deep within the water, the submarine remains calm and still.

Too many Christians are bouncing with the waves because they are like ships on the water rather than submarines having gone deep within the shelter of God's provision, protection, and peace. Until a person marries godliness with contentment, that person will remain vulnerable to the wind and the waves that life frequently stirs up.

Sure, I understand that contentment can be elusive. It's not something we naturally possess. That's why Paul informed us in the book of Philippians that he had to learn contentment. He had to grow out of feelings of discontentment through various life lessons. Life is a master instructor and those who pay attention can gain from the many lessons it has to teach. Paul wrote that contentment provided him with the freedom to move within the space of life's many changes. We read,

> Not that I speak from want, for I have learned to be content
> in whatever circumstances I am. I know how to get along with
> humble means, and I also know how to live in prosperity; in any
> and every circumstance I have learned the secret of being filled
> and going hungry, both of having abundance and suffering need.
> PHILIPPIANS 4:11-12

Paul gives us a glimpse into the art of living with contentment by spanning the breadth of circumstances. He said he learned to be content with more than enough but also without nearly enough. First, he had to learn to be content without much at all. The great gain God offers us doesn't always apply to financial wealth. It is the true riches I wrote about earlier. These come in the way of future reward or present graces such as peace, joy, and a greater experience of Him.

But not only did Paul have to learn how to be content with little, he also had to learn how to be content with much. Now, that may surprise many people to see that Paul had to learn to be content with more than enough. But it shouldn't surprise us. A tendency exists as people accumulate more and more and nicer and nicer to want even more and more and even nicer and nicer. Greed breeds greater greed.

Some of the happiest and most content people on the planet live in the most impoverished countries. Poverty does not preclude contentment. And wealth is not a natural antidote for discontentment. In fact, affluence often contributes to the increase of discontentment. Yet Paul said he learned to be content with little and with much. He allowed the process of change between lack and abundance to instruct him on what matters most—a focus on God as the Source and definition of all.

> *When a person has much, it opens up the doors to a greater desire for much more. But what lack will teach you is gratitude.*

When a person has much, it opens up the doors to a greater desire for much more. But what lack will teach you is gratitude. Recently, I had to preach a sermon on Sunday in my tennis shoes. Now, if you've ever attended the church where I pastor, you will know that we dress up to go to church. Men often wear suits and ties, and dress shoes. I always do. That is, unless I'm suffering from arthritic pain in my foot like I did one particular Sunday.

Due to the excruciating pain, I had to forgo the nice, name-brand dress shoes and wear what would allow me to move around despite reduced mobility. My circumstances reminded me on that day what really matters most when it comes to shoes. I didn't have the luxury of choosing which fancy shoes to wear. All that mattered was comfort. God will often allow lack in a person's life to teach them this important lesson of what matters most. The fact that I could wear shoes at all was a delight to me. The fact that I could stand and walk brought me gratitude. It is often easier to live with contentment and gratefulness when we are limited by life's circumstances because it is easier to discern what truly matters most.

Learning contentment in lack and in abundance was Paul's urging to Timothy. Paul had learned the secret—which was found in understanding and embracing his sufficiency in Jesus Christ. The writer of Hebrews puts it this way:

> Make sure that your character is free from the love of money, being content with what you have; for He Himself has said, "I will never desert you, nor will I ever forsake you," so that we confidently say, "The LORD is my helper, I will not be afraid. What will man do to me?"
>
> HEBREWS 13:5-6

Being content with what you have sets you free to recognize the Source of all things—Jesus Christ. He will never leave you. He will never forsake you. He is the unseen resource of all that you need. Yes, you may want more, but discovering the secret of contentment in what you have keeps your perspective where it needs to be: on Jesus. Notice the connection in the passage above between contentment and Jesus' presence in our lives: Jesus has promised to never forsake you, but that promise comes in the context of your contentment. When you are satisfied in Him, you tap into all He has to provide for you when you need it.

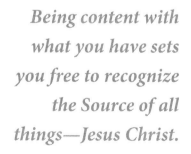

Being content with what you have sets you free to recognize the Source of all things—Jesus Christ.

The reason this must be your mindset is that you brought nothing into the world and you are going to take nothing out of the world. Whatever material items you have in the here and now are not eternal. More important than that, they are not what matters most.

I'm reminded of the story of the businessman who visited Mexico for a vacation. He came across a man fishing along the shore. As the businessman was trying to de-stress from his hectic life, he noticed the fisherman pulling in an enormous yellowfin tuna. The sheer size of the fish got his business gears turning so he went down to visit with the fisherman.

> *When you become a slave to bills for things you don't really need rather than being a free person basking in your gratitude of God's provision, you have fallen prey to the world's perspective.*

The businessman explained to him that if he set up a system whereby he could catch a significant number of these large tuna, he could export and sell them for great profit.

The businessman with his MBA from Harvard went over a growth strategy that included buying boats, establishing a fishery, and creating a brand. After he finished his long-winded pitch to the fisherman, the fisherman asked him why he would want to do all of that. The businessman thought the answer to that question was simple, "Because in around twenty years you will have grown your business sales into the millions so that you can then retire with enough money in order to spend time with your family, do what you love, and enjoy daily siestas."

The fisherman just smiled and shook his head. "I already spend time with my family, do what I love, and enjoy daily siestas," he said. Then he walked away with the tuna he had caught for his family's dinner.

What the world will cause you to think is that you can expand at the cost of what matters most. Yet all the while you simply climb a high ladder only to discover it was leaning against the wrong wall. Godliness with contentment already provides you with great gain. Jesus has all you need to live freely and fully in the satisfaction of His abundant supply.

I'm not saying it's wrong to want a bigger house or a nicer car, but it becomes wrong when those desires morph into obsessions at the cost of your spiritual priorities. When you become a slave to bills for things you don't really need rather than being a free person basking in your gratitude of God's provision, you have fallen prey to the world's perspective. It is only in marrying contentment with godliness that you will open the pathway for God to come to your aid. That is the mindset and perspective of a kingdom steward.

Money Matters

Returning to Paul's earlier instruction to Timothy, he takes us further along in our understanding of the proper perspective on money. In 1 Timothy 6:9-10, Paul states, "But those who want to get rich fall into temptation and a snare and many foolish and harmful desires which plunge men into ruin and destruction. For the love of money is a root of all sorts of evil, and some by longing for it have wandered away from the faith and pierced themselves with many griefs."

In this passage, Paul raises the concept of the longing to be rich. What's important to distinguish here first is that God does not condemn being rich. What is being condemned is a wrongly-placed desire for riches. Ecclesiastes 5:10 states, "He who loves money will not be satisfied with money, nor he who loves abundance with its income. This too is vanity." It's not money that produces the snare that leads to destruction. It's the love of money that produces it. Without contentment, the love of money will lead a person down the path to ruin and all sorts of evil. This is because once a person loves money, Satan has their number. He has duped them.

How do you know if you love money? One way you can answer that question is if you are making more of it yet enjoying it less. Or if you are using money in ungodly ways. Another way to know you love money is that you are spending more time complaining than giving thanks. If your financial life is going up but your spiritual life is going down, then you have become ensnared by the love and pursuit of money. A misplaced value in the love of money is revealed when a person prays more for cash than for a better character, or when a person treats people with money better than those without it, or when a person robs God to spend on themselves.

As we have seen elsewhere in this book, God is not opposed to money. In fact, God Himself gives you and me the power to make wealth. But what God is opposed to is when you look to money as your source. The moment money becomes your source, it also becomes your love. That's the point when the devil has ensnared you, and your love of money will now lead you to the accumulation of all kinds of grief.

I've conducted marital counseling sessions for decades and money is the number one reason for arguments and discord in marriages. Families pile up debt seeking to keep up with the Joneses in buying things they do not need with money they do not have in order to impress people they do not know. This becomes a repetitious cycle so that even when your income goes up, your debt goes up as well. Why? Because you are trapped in the snare of the love of money. You got duped by the devil. God is your Source. He is also to be your first love. If you choose to let money be your primary focus in life, God will let you. He will also let you experience the consequences as the devil brings greater misery into your life.

Many people are not aware that the devil can bless you with money. He can increase your storehouse. But the devil's blessings are not like God's blessings. When God blesses, He says that He adds no sorrow to it (Proverbs 10:22). But when the devil makes people rich, he traps them with the very stuff he blessed them with. Before long, what was perceived to be a blessing really morphs into a curse, revealing the true intention of the snare all along.

This reminds me of the story of the man who called his pastor to ask for prayer. He explained how he had been extremely happy years before when he was only making $30,000 a year. But now that he was making $200,000 a year, everything was piling up as stress in his life. The pastor agreed to pray for him. "Father," the pastor began, "please take this man back to $30,000 a year in income so that he can be happy again."

I'm sure that was not the prayer the man was asking for but it was the prayer the pastor knew he had to pray. Falling in love with money and all that money can obtain is the root of a lot of conflict, stress, worry, greed, busy schedules, and a lack of contentment. All of this leads to loss in satisfaction, peace, and the full experience of God's presence.

Yes, you are to maximize your life and the skills God has given to you. But you are never to fall in love with what it brings your way. The moment the spiritual becomes secondary to the material in your value system, you have now invited God to exit your environment. This is the core problem of Prosperity Theology, the theology where God exists to make everybody rich, and where the church is somehow to operate as a divine slot machine. God never guarantees that everyone will be rich. What He promises is that He will meet your needs. He will never forsake you. He will never abandon you. And He can supply you with things far more valuable than money—things like peace, hope, and authentic joy.

It is a kingdom steward's perspective that merits great gain. When

> *Yes, you are to maximize your life and the skills God has given to you. But you are never to fall in love with what it brings your way.*

godliness and contentment join forces in your soul, you will reap the benefits of their fruit.

Acts of Kindness

My wife and I recently took a trip to Kenya to minister there among a local body of Christ. This trip served as a stark and visual reminder of how truly rich we are in our nation. Did you know that if you have a household income of over $34,000, you are considered to be in the top one percent of income in the world? What that means is that you make more money than 99 percent of the world's inhabitants. Sure, you may not feel "rich" according to our nation's standards but, according to the world and its median levels of income, you are rich.

So, I think it is safe to say that the next verse we are going to study will apply to most people reading this book right now. Paul continues his discussion on great gain in 1 Timothy 6:17-19:

> Instruct those who are rich in this present world not to be
> conceited or to fix their hope on the uncertainty of riches, but
> on God, who richly supplies us with all things to enjoy. Instruct
> them to do good, to be rich in good works, to be generous and
> ready to share, storing up for themselves the treasure of a good
> foundation for the future, so that they may take hold of that
> which is life indeed.

In these verses, Paul gives Timothy, as well as all of us who read and study the Scriptures, a mindset of kingdom stewardship. Paul takes a moment to give instructions for the rich because the wrong view of wealth only leads to ruin. To be rich means to have an abundance beyond that which is needed to meet your personal or family needs for food, clothes, and shelter. It is clear from this passage that God is not against the righteous acquisition, use, and enjoyment of His gracious provision. In fact, the Bible is full of people to whom God gave great wealth (Adam, Job, Solomon, Moses, Daniel, and others). However, those who are rich are not to be conceited. That means they are not to get the big head. Wealth has side effects, and one of those side effects is arrogance. Wealth can literally make you think more of yourself than you ought. Never let your net worth confuse you about your self-worth because unless your identity is rooted in Christ, you are not living out the full potential of your self-worth. The amount of money in your bank account or investment portfolio, the number

Never let your net worth confuse you about your self-worth because unless your identity is rooted in Christ, you are not living out the full potential of your self-worth.

of cars in your garage, and the variety of vacations posted on your social media accounts do not determine your value. Your value rises through a greater reflection of the true character and heart of Jesus Christ.

Far too many people confuse net worth with spiritual influence. We had a member in our church years ago who was extremely wealthy. After a while, he approached me about becoming a leader in the church. I explained the extensive process we have in place for becoming a spiritual leader in our church, and he simply smiled. "Oh," he said, "I understand that is your normal process, but I don't think you understand, Pastor, that I can do a lot for your church."

I calmly told the man that I did understand and appreciated his eagerness, but he would still have to go through the over-a-year-long training program to become a leader. That's when he hit me with the big one. He replied, "Tony, there are a lot of churches all over this community who would love to have me as a leader in their church."

I paused, kept a lid on my composure, and then politely replied, "Well, then, you had better start visiting those churches."

What this man had wanted to do was use his money to buy influence illegitimately. Now, I'm not saying that money is bad. Money is a primary means that God uses to expand ministry and enable us to do all we do to impact lives for God's kingdom. But when someone confuses their intrinsic value with their income, that's when money twists things. A spiritual leader is someone who serves humbly with grace, diligence, and integrity. A spiritual leader is not someone who seeks to skirt the process by buying his way up the ladder.

Another situation came up when we were building our church years ago and had four contractors bid on the multi-million-dollar expansion. Each contractor submitted a proposal and gave a presentation to our building committee. However, following one presentation, the contractor called me personally to talk privately. He explained that he could set up an account in my name and put $250,000 in that account as a rebate back to me if I chose to go with them. What they were asking was that I would use my clout as senior pastor to sway the committee to choose them, and in return, they would reward me richly. Two hundred and fifty thousand dollars is a lot of money but in 1995, when this happened, it was an even more enormous sum.

We are never to fix our hopes on the uncertainty or arrogance of riches. Rather, we are to firmly fix our hopes on God.

Needless to say, that contractor didn't get the contract. The kingdom of God is not for sale. You and I are not to profit off of God's kingdom illegitimately. Paul was urging Timothy, and everyone who reads his words, to adopt an attitude of service, humility, and generosity. Not conceit, manipulation, and hoarding.

We are never to fix our hopes on the uncertainty or arrogance of riches. Rather, we are to firmly fix our hopes on God. Since God is the owner and He is the Source, we are to look to Him alone for all things. Yes, God uses business to produce profits. Yes, God grants opportunities and opens doors. Yes, God can maximize a person's education or expertise. What this passage is saying is that we are not to fix our hope, love, or value on money. When we do, we have confused money as the source when God is the real Source of all.

If you get seriously sick, money alone can't fix that. If you lose your mind or peace, money can't fix that. If your relationships are falling apart, money can't fix that. Money has its place, yes. But it is not the source of all you need. God is.

There will be a time in everyone's life when God is the only One who can fix what they are facing. That's why it is critical to keep God in His rightful place as we steward all He has provided for us to manage. He is the Source. We are not to set our heart on riches (Psalm 62:10).

Now, it's okay to enjoy whatever God gives you. If you have abundance, it's okay to have it. If you obtained it legitimately and are using it righteously, you are to enjoy it. But in order to maximize your enjoyment you must learn, as Paul did, the secret of contentment. Contentment understands that God is the One who opened the doors and paved the way for you to have what you have.

> *Far too many believers with means spend far too much time enjoying God's generosity and far too little time using His divinely bestowed gifts of time, talents, and treasures to minister to others and advance His agenda as His kingdom stewards.*

Contentment also understands that God gets to choose the use of what He's given to you.

As Paul instructs us in this passage, those who are rich are to be rich in good works. Those who are blessed are to be a blessing to others. If God has shown you favor, you are to leverage what He's given to you for the benefit of others and the advancement of His kingdom. God expects you to use what you have to help others. It's not all about you. Far too many believers with means spend far too much time enjoying God's generosity and far too little time using His divinely bestowed gifts of time, talents, and treasures to minister to others and advance His agenda as His kingdom stewards. If more time is spent enjoying God's wealth than using it for good works, then things are out of balance. A higher net worth should result in a greater level of giving and serving since to whom much is given, much is required (Luke 12:48). In fact, if you have been granted by God a high net worth, you should look into such things as real estate, partnership investments, tax-deferred trusts, and the like in order to increase your capacity for greater generosity.

> *When you multiply acts of kindness by the myriads of people blessed by God through His church, there is more than enough love, generosity, care, prayer, and even food to go around.*

One of the favorite ministries we have at our church is the ministry of kindness. We developed "Acts of Kindness" cards for all members to pick up and deliver to those in need. They have the name and address of the church on them and provide a way for us to reach out to help others while connecting it back to the spiritual. Not long ago, I ran across a homeless man and he came up to me to tell me he was very hungry. I took a moment to buy him some food and when I gave it to him, I also asked if I could pray with him. He agreed to have me pray with him and after I prayed, I handed him the card and explained that if he needed any further help, he could call the number on the card.

When you multiply acts of kindness by the myriads of people blessed by God through His church, there is more than enough love, generosity, care, prayer, and even food to go around. As followers of Jesus Christ, we ought to be looking for opportunities to spread kindness in His name. That's the mindset of a kingdom steward. Kingdom stewards are to be about the business of generosity. Paul said plainly, "Instruct them to do good, to be rich in good works, to be generous and ready to share, storing up for themselves the treasure of a good foundation for the future, so that they may take hold of that which is life indeed" (1 Timothy 6:18-19).

As we saw in the chapter on strategy, it is in doing good works through acts of generosity that you will store up for yourself a good foundation for the future. Every time you choose to use your time, talents, or treasures to do a good work for God and His glory, you are making a deposit into your own storage account for eternity. God puts something in your off-site storage unit, awaiting your arrival in heaven. And when you arrive to meet God face-to-face one day in heaven, He's not going to ask you how much you made or what your annual salary was. He won't inquire about your net worth. Or even what degree you earned. But He will check to see how much you have stored up in heaven based on how you managed what He gave you on earth.

> *By investing what you have now through generous, humble service, you will take hold of that which is life indeed.*

By investing what you have now through generous, humble service, you will take hold of that which is life indeed. The word "indeed" means "for real." God has stated that He will offer you a trade. If you use what He has given to you on earth the way He has prescribed for you to use it, keeping Him as your Source in a spirit and mindset of contentment, He will give you the kind of life that is "for real." You won't just be getting by. You will be living the abundant life Jesus provides (John 10:10). Not only will you have a storage unit full to the brim in heaven, but you will have ongoing access to the spiritual riches from the Source of all strength, peace, wisdom, insight, emotional stability, and more while on earth. As we use earth to lay up treasures in heaven, not only will our hearts be realigned to a greater eternal focus, but we will simultaneously be decreasing the temptation to allow money to become our master that will lead to a decrease in the spiritual experience of God's reality in our lives and the true riches He offers (Matthew 6:19-20), including overcoming the sin of worry (Matthew 6:25-34).

As we close this chapter, can I ask you to do me a favor sometime this week? Will you just take a moment to visit a nearby junkyard? I just want you to gaze out over all the discarded furniture, belongings, and once-treasured items. I want you to look at the junkyard as a reminder of where everything on earth winds up. Never ever put your hope, value, or joy in stuff. It's just going to end up in the junkyard. Remember, while you can't take it with you—you can forward it ahead (2 Timothy 4:6-8).

Rather, put your hope in the goodness of God and His ability to maximize your time, talents, and treasures to create a kingdom impact. Keep your perspective on Him and on knowing Him more fully. When you place your hope in the steadfastness of God as your Source, you will discover the secret of contentment, the power of gratitude, and the freeing peace of true generosity as God's kingdom steward.

9

PROFESSION

All of us have a kingdom over which we rule. It might be a three-bedroom kingdom. It could be a four-bedroom kingdom with an office. Or it could be an apartment-kingdom. Whatever the case, we run and rule our home environment. Men or women have been known to say, "I am the king of my castle," or "I am the queen of my home."

In each of our kingdoms, we have servants. All of us do. They are called appliances. These servants are designed to do what we do not want to do for ourselves in the running of our kingdom. The refrigerator keeps things cold. The stove makes things hot. The toaster browns the bread. Electric can openers open the cans. The furnace warms the home in the winter. You get the point. All of these are servants in our respective kingdoms.

Now, one of the frustrating things is when those servants aren't serving well. When the appliances aren't doing what they were meant to achieve, either because they are broken or because they are not working to their full potential, that causes our kingdom to not live up to our expectations. I recently went to get a cup of coffee and the Keurig only released a third of the entire cup. Apparently, the rest of the water got trapped somewhere in the process. You can be assured that I was not happy with this at all. Maybe you've gone through something similar.

You look at the item that is supposed to accomplish one task, and you wonder why it can't do the one thing it was designed to do.

Well, I wonder if that is how God feels about us sometimes. After all, we live in His kingdom and He has created each of us with a specific destiny and purpose to fulfill. God expects us to faithfully oversee the time, talents, and treasures He's given to us according to the manner of our own unique calling. One of the primary ways this is done is through our work. The purpose of work, from a kingdom perspective, is the protection and expansion of all that God has placed within your realm of influence.

> *God instituted the concept of work before sin ever entered the world.*

In fact, the concept of work is rooted in all things good. God instituted the concept of work before sin ever entered the world. When there was a perfect world and a perfect environment, there existed perfect work. He originally set it up as a partnership between Himself and the worker. They were to utilize the creative genius God had deposited within them as bearers of His image. Males and females were to tackle the needs and development of all of creation together. God began by placing Adam in the garden with the instruction to cultivate it and keep it. He put Adam to work. He also gave Adam the responsibility of naming the species of every animal in His entire creation (Genesis 2:19). From early on, humanity has been entrusted with a significant role. This is your job; your profession. Therefore, work and God are intricately connected.

What we are looking at in this chapter is a theology of work, not a sociology of work. As a kingdom steward, theology is interwoven into all aspects of what you do. Stewardship includes much more than just what you choose to put in the offering plate at church. Stewardship includes every decision you make. And since most of us spend the bulk of our waking hours at work pursuing our career goals, much of our stewardship responsibility is carried out on the job. Without a biblical understanding of work, most people will waste the preeminent method they have been given to serve and honor God.

Our look at the theology of work begins in the garden. Before sin, there existed no definition of work where God was not included. God was always a partner in the work. Work was God's prescribed way of partnering with mankind in the process of exercising dominion. Work is divinely designed to produce goods and services through the righteous cultivation and development of the earth's resources for the glory of God, the good of mankind, and the expansion of His kingdom.

Productive work is one of the primary means of fulfilling the Creation mandate for us to exercise dominion over His creation. It is also the divinely authorized means to financial stability (Proverbs 12:11-12). Refusing to work or seeking to gain wealth through manipulation, dishonesty, or get-rich-quick schemes are all greatly condemned in Scripture (Proverbs 13:11; 15:27; 20:10, 23; 28:19-20; 2 Thessalonians 3:11-12). But all legitimate human work is dependent on the work that God has already done in creation. We must never forget that our work is sourced by and dependent on God's work since all productivity is dependent upon the provisions God has already deposited in creation. This even includes the oxygen necessary for mankind to do any work at all.

> *He gave us a Sabbath rest as well to allow time for the enjoyment of His creation.*

God also placed a reminder in the center of the garden that He was not to be left out of work. That reminder was the tree of the knowledge of good and evil. Rather than turn to a separate source for insight, Adam was to rely on God for His direction since God was the Creator and knew the path he should take.

In addition to the centrality of God in every aspect of work, God also instituted a day of rest and enjoyment. God did not rest on the seventh day because He was tired; He rested to fully enjoy what He had done all week long. Thus, He gave us a Sabbath rest as well to allow time for the enjoyment of His creation.

We see this day of rest being brought up throughout Scripture in various ways. When the Israelites wandered in the wilderness, they were commanded to gather manna for six days. And on the sixth day, they were to gather enough for two days so that one day a week would be devoted to rest, enjoyment, and the worship of God (Exodus 16:22-26). One day a week was set apart for the entirety of God's people to remember that He is the Source. There existed no job, salary, or economics apart from God.

In New Testament times, we read about a rest given to God's people. It's not limited to a certain day of the week as Colossians 2:16 reminds us, but the overarching principle remains. It is a system by which rest reminds us regularly that our work and productivity is not to exist independently of God. The Sabbath day also assists us in breaking the power of coveting in our hearts while simultaneously helping to disconnect us from an unhealthy focus on earning more money.

The Curse

The concept of work was created in the pure environment of the garden with specific rules and an ordained rest. Yet things changed when sin entered the world—with sin came the curse. We read in Genesis 3:17-18,

> Then to Adam He said, "Because you have listened to the voice of your wife, and have eaten from the tree about which I commanded you, saying, 'You shall not eat from it'; cursed is the ground because of you; in toil you will eat of it all the days of your life. Both thorns and thistles it shall grow for you; and you will eat the plants of the field."

As a result of sin, we now live and work in a cursed environment. That reality must come into play when we look at the theology of work. How do we carry out our tasks within an atmosphere predisposed toward conflicts and disappointments? The curse brought with it "thorns and thistles" that we still have to contend with today.

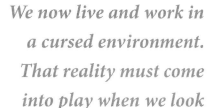

We now live and work in a cursed environment. That reality must come into play when we look at the theology of work.

While most of us are no longer farmers dealing with literal thorns and thistles, these trials and impediments still exist in other forms. Some of you dread going to work because you don't like your job. Or perhaps you don't like the people you have to work with. Or you are praying that God will relocate your supervisor or boss. Still others live for the office, thus turning their job and the profit it brings into an idol.

Studies show that work-related stress is the highest contributor to stress in American adults. A recent nationwide analysis revealed that over 40 percent of workers said their work was "extremely stressful." And over 80 percent said that their work produced internal stress at some level.[1]

The curse is clearly still alive and well. And sin remains the culprit. When Adam and Eve first separated from God, they ushered in a curse on employment. What had originally been intended as an easy and natural cultivation of creation turned into a frustrating task of fighting soil littered with thorns and thistles. In today's culture, we still fight the thorns and thistles of demands, personalities, and competition. This new variety of consequences carry out the same effect as they stick you, prick you, cut you, irritate you, and cause you to lose joy in your job.

One of the major reasons we still get stressed under the weight of sin's consequences is because most of us still disconnect God from our work. We do not seek to partner with Him in our careers. We look to ourselves and our own understanding of how to navigate difficult people, overcome unrealistic expectations, and find calm in the midst of competition. Only God's wisdom and power can overcome the curse. Yet when we dismiss Him from the overarching rule in our careers, we also dismiss His involvement for good.

Far too many view work as another god. It's an idol. They may worship God on Sunday but worship another god on Monday. How do I know it's worship? Because the essence of worship is attention, affection, dedication, and loyalty. When your career gets your best efforts and highest thoughts, over and above God, it has become an idol. God must remain preeminent, even over your work. He doesn't want you and me to whistle while we work, He wants us to worship Him while we work. Work was never intended to become disconnected from God.

Multiple thorns and thistles have grown up in the workplace due to this bifurcation of the sacred and the secular. For starters, we have the thorn of injustice where people are put in work environments that are simply not fair or safe. These are oppressive forces of labor and they exist worldwide. Systems of slavery and servitude that keep people from fulfilling and maximizing their gifts and calling under God and force them to support unrighteous activities or systems in order to survive are evil at their core. Job decries the evil oppression taking place due to the separation of God from work (Job 24:4-11). And in 1 Samuel 8:11-18, we read about the government putting people in positions of forced labor. These are just a few biblical examples of what has too regularly taken place due to sin invading the marketplace.

> *Multiple thorns and thistles have grown up in the workplace due to this bifurcation of the sacred and the secular.*

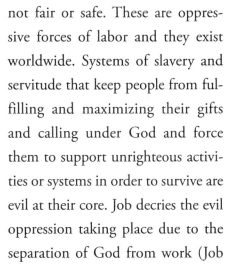

Another thistle is that of greed. Greed is the materialistic disposition of the mind and heart whereby people seek to accumulate goods, money, position, and power illegitimately or at the expense of the well-being, safety, and benefit of others. It is the illegitimate and unauthorized pursuit, desire, and acquisition of material gain. Greed is driven by the mindset that you are what you possess, turning money into an idolatrous master (Matthew 6:24). Greed and idolatry go hand in hand (Colossians 3:5). Greed is where the physical and financial take precedence over the spiritual and eternal, leading to the reversal of kingdom priorities (Matthew 6:33). When God gets separated from work, then individuals and businesses can easily fall prey to misusing people for profit. Countless people suffer in today's economy due to the unregulated advances in our food, energy, and technology. Not to mention the negative impact on our natural environment and animals.

Ecclesiastes 2:17-24 reminds us that when God gets separated from work, vanity sets in. Work becomes nothing more than the production of money in the pursuit of pleasure and power. Another form of greed is predatory lending, which has occurred across all history and cultures, distorting the blessing work was originally intended to supply. In Nehemiah 5:1-8, we read about the poor having to borrow money with exorbitant interest rates that kept them oppressed.

A third thistle we often face in work today is the thistle of mismanagement of employees by employers. Deuteronomy 24:14 says, "You shall not oppress a hired servant who is poor and needy, whether he is one of your countrymen or one of your aliens who is in your land in your towns." God strictly imposed a system of fair treatment of employees by employers. Yet when employers separate God and His principles from the workplace, fairness doesn't always exist. James 5:4 condemns the employer who holds out on his employees by not paying them their just wages on time. In fact, Scripture condemns economic systems that have been set up with a centralized approach to profit. Revelation 13:16-17 reveals that a centralized economic system is the economic system of the anti-Christ. Thus, top-down governments with over-taxation and a myriad of other illegitimate economic practices and regulations are rooted in the principles and precepts of Satan himself.

A fourth thistle is laziness and irresponsibility. This includes those who refuse to be productive and as a result live in unnecessary poverty and dependency on other people, churches, or the government. Such sluggardness is condemned by God and is an insult to any claim of a Christian to be a kingdom steward (Proverbs 13:4; 20:4).

Take God to Work Day

So, with the curse in full force throughout our careers all across our nation and the world, how can a person find meaning, value, and enjoyment in work? Is it even possible to do so while operating in a cursed environment? The answer to that question is a resounding yes, and you do so by reconnecting what got disconnected. You have to bring God's perspective to bear in everything you do at work. When you go to work, you have to take God with you. Invite His will, rule, and authority to have full reign over your thoughts, actions, and reactions. In other words, your work is part of your kingdom stewardship responsibility.

When you go to work, you have to take God with you. Invite His will, rule, and authority to have full reign over your thoughts, actions, and reactions.

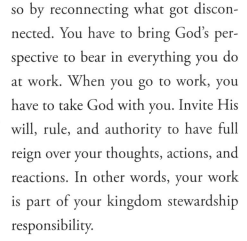

Every fourth Thursday of April, we have in our country what is called "Take Our Daughters and Sons to Work Day." This is an annual event where employees can bring their children with them to work. It is designed to expand the minds of the youth and expose them to a greater worldview on work. Well, God doesn't want to just join you on the fourth Thursday of every April. Unfortunately, one day a year is about how often He gets to join many people at work, though. To live as a kingdom steward in your career, you have to adopt the mentality of taking God with you to work every single day.

The apostle Paul gives us the framework for how we are to successfully live this out. Keep in mind, the cultural context in which he wrote his letter to the church at Colossae was that of rampant slavery. They were in the Roman Empire, and half of the Roman population were slaves. Slavery wasn't a job someone would go apply for. It was a reality that the people were forced to live in. Thus, when we read Paul's insights on work, we discover the spiritual approach to serving even in undesirable working conditions. Granted, slaves were forced to serve, whereas when we work in our careers, our service is given in exchange for an income. But the foundational biblical worldview of serving remains the same in both scenarios.

We read in Colossians 3:22-24,

Slaves, in all things obey those who are your masters on earth, not with external service, as those who merely please men, but with sincerity of heart, fearing the Lord. Whatever you do, do your work heartily, as for the Lord rather than for men, knowing that from the Lord you will receive the reward of the inheritance. It is the Lord Christ whom you serve.

This passage clearly reveals what is the predominant issue for most believers in the workplace. Far too many are working for the wrong person. They are working for the wrong boss, supervisor, or manager. Scripture says that when you and I go to work, we are to work for the Lord. We are to serve the Lord. Yes, we may have an earthly boss but in God's kingdom economy, they are the middle managers. He is the Boss. You work for God. Therefore, you and I are never to settle for mediocrity in our work. Rather, we are to strive for the highest degree and standard of excellence since the God we serve is excellent and expects the same from His image-bearers (2 Samuel 22:31-33; Psalm 8:1).

When you go to work each day, you need to keep that in mind. You are to throw yourself into what you do in total dedication because you serve the King of kings. You are to bring His mindset into your workday decisions. You are to seek His blessing and direction on the work of your hands. God wants you to change your whole line of thinking about the work you do, the business you run, and the investments that you manage. They are to be as a sacred responsibility, even in a sacred environment. You and I are not to view ourselves as the final boss of our lives or our resources.

It's true that the first Adam disconnected work from God when he sinned, but the last Adam, Jesus Christ (1 Corinthians 15:45), reconnected God with work. In Luke 4:16-21 Jesus speaks from Isaiah 61. He shares the good news for the oppressed, marginalized, and over-worked. He speaks of the "favorable year of the LORD" where all debts were removed. This is the Year of Jubilee as referenced in Leviticus 25. The Year of Jubilee was a time for societal reset. All slaves were set free. All properties were returned to their original family or owner so that there could be generational wealth and not multigenerational poverty. God brought good news in this year by restoring societal, economic, and employment disparities back to the state of their original intent.

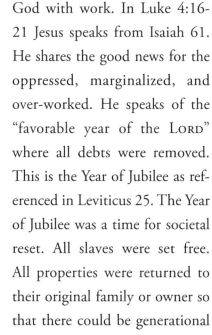

God wants you to change your whole line of thinking about the work you do, the business you run, and the investments that you manage. They are to be as a sacred responsibility.

When Jesus came on the scene, He said that He brought this jubilee in Himself. He came to set us free—free from the bondage of sin and the consequences it brings. We access this gift of freedom and abundant life Jesus came to give by aligning our lives under His overarching rule.

Colossians 3:17 states it this way, "Whatever you do in word or deed, do all in the name of the Lord Jesus, giving thanks through Him to God the Father." That verse doesn't say whatever you do on Sunday, do all in the name of the Lord Jesus. No, it says "whatever you do." Period. That means you do not only worship God on Sunday. You worship God on Monday, Tuesday, Wednesday, Thursday, Friday, and Saturday as well. You worship Him through your work when you bring His perspective and rule into all of your thoughts, decisions, actions, and words. And you worship Him when you give thanks to Him, through Jesus, for everything He has allowed to come across your path. Living as a kingdom steward with this perspective changes everything.

One man saw a guy laying bricks and he went over to ask him what he was doing. The man replied, "Oh, I'm laying bricks. I'm a bricklayer." He then went over to another man doing the same thing and asked what he was doing. "I'm building a cathedral," came his reply. Sure, all he was doing was laying bricks but he saw something more than the job set before him.

If all you see is your profession, you don't see enough. You have to look further than that. You have to recognize what you are doing for God through the job that you have. As we read in Colossians 3:24, "It is the Lord Christ whom you serve." In your heart, mind, and perspective, you must remember that you work for and serve God. That doesn't mean you go and tell your boss on the job that you have another boss. I'm not trying to get you in trouble. What that does mean is that you filter everything through the lens of God's perspective.

You serve your earthly boss and perform your earthly responsibilities as if unto the Lord Himself, which means you do your job with excellence and integrity. Keep in mind, Paul wrote this passage to slaves in Rome. No doubt they had stress on the job. But changing the perspective of who you are ultimately serving can reduce that stress because God ties eternal rewards as well as spiritual and physical blessings in the here and now to how well you serve Him.

A kingdom steward always remembers that the spiritual is directly connected to the physical, especially in the area of work. That means a doctor is not just a doctor, but also God's representative in the medical field so that the medical field sees what God looks like when He helps hurting people. It means a lawyer is not just a lawyer, he or she is God's representative in the bar association so that the bar association sees what God looks like when He tries a case. It means a homemaker is more than a homemaker; she is God's representative in the home demonstrating what God looks like in managing a well-run home. A retail worker is not just a retail worker, she or he is to reflect God's image and values in the retail establishment space through revealing a spirit of kindness, patience, and generosity. It means a schoolteacher is more than a schoolteacher, she or he is God's manager in the classroom demonstrating what God looks like when He imparts knowledge. It means that the trash collector isn't just a trash collector but a person working with God to help stop the spread of disease. In other words, your career is one of the platforms God has given you to bring good to others and glory to God, thus advancing His kingdom agenda. Therefore you must "kingdomize" your work.

You serve your earthly boss and perform your earthly responsibilities as if unto the Lord Himself, which means you do your job with excellence and integrity.

In the same way, your career also gives you the opportunity to lay up eternal treasures.

Stop leaving God at church. Take Him to work. He wants to be a part of the widgets you are making, letters you are typing, businesses you are building, and entrepreneurial risk you are taking. He wants to be a part of the education you are pursuing. He wants to climb the ladder with you.

Work is a way to provide for yourself and for your family. To not work, if you are physically able to do so, is to go against God's will for your life (1 Timothy 5:8). The Bible states plainly that if a person doesn't work, he ought not to eat (2 Thessalonians 3:10). Your responsibility is to work, whether that is in a paid position or in the role of caring for the needs of the home (Titus 2:5). Work also offers you the opportunity to give to supporting God's ongoing work of ministry for the proclamation of the gospel as well as the spiritual growth and discipleship of the saints (Matthew 28:18-20; Luke 8:1-3; Philippians 4:15-19). In Deuteronomy 24:19, God told the business people of that day not to harvest everything they produced. They were instructed to leave margin behind for the poor to glean. The edges of their farms were to remain unharvested so that those who did not have means for farming could have the opportunity to work for their food.

In our contemporary culture, we are to also leave margin for giving in what we earn from our work (Leviticus 19:9-10; Ephesians 4:28) in order to help others, especially if they are poor and oppressed (Isaiah 58:6-12; James 1:27). God promises to bless such a commitment. After all, we are all gleaners in God's field. It is equally important for Christian employers to recognize that they are to be kingdom stewards in how they treat their employees. Their master in heaven will hold them accountable for this sacred duty (Colossians 4:1). In addition, we should determine before God how much is enough so that the surplus can be used for the expansion of kingdom impact, resulting in the exponential increase of our kingdom reward (Mark 10:29-30). If God has given you a special capacity to make money, then you must seriously consider whether He has also given you the special spiritual gift of giving (Romans 12:8).

Work for the Lord

Psalm 78:72 gives us a process for how we are to go about our work. It says, "So he shepherded them according to the integrity of his heart, and guided them with his skillful hands." This passage speaks to us about David. David functioned with both integrity of heart and skill of hand. In whatever he did, he gave his best effort. We are to approach our work in the same manner. If you are a sanitation worker, God doesn't want you to simply throw a trash can down after emptying it. You are not merely emptying and ridding the location of trash; you are preventing the spread of disease. You are honoring God through honoring the environment in which we all live. You have to think bigger than the action taking place at that moment in time.

> *A person can bring God honor in the humblest of jobs when he or she chooses to include God in it.*

Every legitimate job holds within it the dignity placed in humanity due to being formed in the image of God. Ask God for insight on how your job helps to promote His values on earth, then seek to serve Him with that mindset. A person can bring God honor in the humblest of jobs when he or she chooses to include God in it. When you think from a higher level, which involves skill of hand and integrity of heart, you are now motivated when you go to work. When you operate according to the mindset of a kingdom steward, you know that the promise in Colossians is yours. God will make good on it. He promised. We read it earlier but it's worth repeating so it will become real in your heart and mind, "Whatever you do, do your work heartily, as for the Lord rather than for men, knowing that from the Lord you will receive the reward of the inheritance" (Colossians 3:23-24). It is God from whom you receive the reward for what you do. Men may overlook you. Your boss may pass over you. Other people may get credit for the toil you have done on their behalf. But know beyond a shadow of a doubt that when you work for God, meaning you serve others in a spirit that you are serving Him, He will reward you.

Even if it's work you do not particularly care for, when you work as unto the Lord, you give what Matthew 5:41 calls second-mile service. You don't just go and do what is expected of you. You go beyond it. Why? Because God is worth it. God is worth your effort, attention, and devotion. He wants you to give Him your best. When you do, you can trust Him to take care of your job situation. You can trust Him to turn around your employment scenario. You can trust Him to lift you up when others seek to oppress you or marginalize you, or even misuse you. But you have to take Him on the job with you in order to see Him show up for you. Do remember, however, that God gives you the freedom to change and improve your area of employment when there is the divinely authorized opportunity and desire to do so (1 Corinthians 7:21-22).

James 4 reminds us to always include God in our work plans because we do not even know if tomorrow will be here for us to experience. We read, "You are just a vapor that appears for a little while and then vanishes away. Instead, you ought to say, 'If the Lord wills, we will live and also do this or that.' But as it is, you boast in your arrogance; all such boasting is evil" (verses 14-16). This is a strong warning to businessmen and women never to leave God out just because you think you know what you are doing. Yes, you may have an advanced degree or

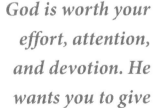

God is worth your effort, attention, and devotion. He wants you to give Him your best.

have satisfied the ten-thousand-hour rule to become an expert in a field. But you may not even make it to the next day, let alone the next hour. Life is a vapor. Don't cut deals, or make your economic projects and plans, without God. It is God who is over all and His rule has the final say in everything.

A great biblical example of this is Daniel. In chapter 6 of the book named after him, we read that Daniel is working for a pagan government. It's an evil empire run by less-than-moral ordinances. Not only that, but due to Daniel's success, he has accrued some haters. He works with some people who simply don't like him and want to get rid of him. A few have their eyes on his title and his clout. So they come up with a scheme to oust Daniel.

The first plot involved finding something wrong with his work. But when they couldn't do that because Daniel was excellent in his performance and above board in his integrity, they came up with another way to trap him. Knowing that Daniel served His God and not the king's gods, they went to the king to pass a law that no one could pray to any other god for thirty days. The king liked this law because it fed his Theo-ego. His own god-complex compelled him to sign a law that said no one could acknowledge or seek any other god but him during the entire month.

Yet when Daniel heard that law, it didn't change his behavior. He still prayed to the one true God as he had always done. Not only that, he didn't seek to hide his prayers either. It says that his windows were open toward Jerusalem as he prayed. Daniel was so certain in what he was doing that he was willing to face the consequences of it head-on. Which he did. Not long after that, the king regretfully had Daniel thrown into the lions' den. The king loved Daniel. He didn't want to throw him into the lions' den, but the law he had signed was irreversible so he had to do it. Yet even though the den was full of hungry lions, when the king went the next day to see if Daniel had survived, Daniel was alive. We read,

God's deliverance rests on your obedience and alignment under Him.

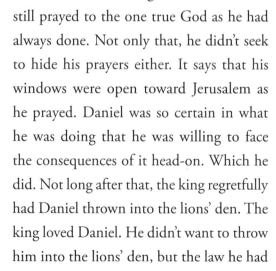

When he [the king] had come near the den to Daniel, he cried
out with a troubled voice. The king spoke and said to Daniel,
"Daniel, servant of the living God, has your God, whom you
constantly serve, been able to deliver you from the lions?"

DANIEL 6:20

Even though the king didn't know the one true God, he still hoped that
He would save Daniel. The fact that the king knew about God from Daniel
also reveals that it was not a secret in Daniel's workplace that he served God.
It was clear to the head of the company that this man was a believer in God
and served God every day at work. He did his work with such extraordinary
excellence, giving God the glory in it, that his beliefs were well known. The
company profited from Daniel's work. As a result, God protected Daniel
in the lions' den. Those hungry lions were his pillow.

The lesson for us is clear: Even if you get fired by your enemies or
if your business gets shut down through no fault of your own, God has
the final say-so. God can turn things around on a dime. In fact, the king
was so relieved that Daniel had survived his night with the lions, he got
all the haters who were hating on Daniel and threw them into the lions'
den instead. And, all of a sudden, those sleepy lions woke up and decided
they had an appetite after all. What's more, Daniel then got a promotion.

I know it may look bleak where you are at right now. I know you may
see no end in sight to whatever challenges you face on the job or with your
business. But when you seek God's blessings in your work and you invite
His perspective into all you do, you will see God turn things around. God
can take from the sinner and give it to the saint (Psalm 105:43-45). He's
just waiting for you to include Him in all you do. God's deliverance rests
on your obedience and alignment under Him.

My friend Tony Dungy would pray with me every week during the
year his team was headed to the Super Bowl. In the week of the actual
Super Bowl, I asked him what he would like for me to pray. He said,

"Tony, this is my request. Whether we win or lose, that I would make God's name great." That was an easy prayer for me to pray on his behalf. Coach Dungy's team did go on to win that Super Bowl, and he became the first African American to coach a team to a win of that magnitude. What impressed me most through the whole experience is how he incorporated God's viewpoint into all he did. And how he used his platform to proclaim his faith.

Sure, you may not be a coach. But that is not the point. If you are a banker, take God to the bank. If you are a grocery store worker, take God to the grocery store. If you are a teacher, take God to school. Wherever you are, include God's perspective in all you do, while simultaneously respecting the governing rules and authorities of your workplace. Be certain to let God's mindset affect your own. When you work as a kingdom steward on your job, God can reverse the curse. God can turn thorns and thistles into an abundance of spiritual treasures. And that all starts by bringing God into every area of your profession. Remember, we are workers together with God (2 Corinthians 6:1).

PART IV

THE
BENEFITS
OF
KINGDOM
STEWARDSHIP

10

REWARDS

Airlines have rewards programs. These are programs designed to get you to fly more by giving you rewards for booking flights and purchasing items from their online shop. Usually you are awarded miles that allow you to fly virtually free due to your ongoing choice of them as your airline provider.

In the world of sports, athletes are offered what are known as incentive clauses. These are clauses designed to increase their productivity by motivating them to accomplish more. More yardage, catches, tackles, or any other detailed item in the incentive clause is rewarded with more money. This serves as motivation to keep the athletes playing at their highest potential throughout the course of a season.

Salvation is free. I don't want to skip over that. Salvation is by grace alone apart from works, through personal faith in the finished work of Jesus Christ and His promise to give eternal life to all who believe in Him for it (Romans 3:24; 4:4-5; Galatians 2:16, 21; Ephesians 2:8-9; Revelation 22:17). You can't buy it, earn it, or work for it because God will only give it away for free. As Titus 3:5 states, "He saved us, not on the basis of deeds which we have done in righteousness, but according to His mercy, by the washing of regeneration and renewing by the Holy Spirit."

But once a person is born again, God has an incentive clause. He has a rewards program. Keep in mind, the rewards program has nothing to do with the security of your eternal destiny because that's a free gift from God. But the rewards program has everything to do with how much of heaven you get to experience on earth as well as your kingdom inheritance when you get to glory. God's rewards program, unlike eternal salvation, is based on a faith that works—not faith apart from works (James 2:14-21).

God wants you to maximize your potential on earth and to increase His engagement with your life. He seeks to do this by incentivizing what you do. In fact, God has laid out seven specific incentives for you to aim for as you manage the time, talents, and treasures He has placed within your realm of kingdom stewardship. These seven potential rewards do not come to believers simply because they are Christians. It's only when you, as a kingdom steward, rightly position yourself in God's kingdom program through the choices you make that they will be made available to you. These make up some of the key abundant life benefits that Jesus offers to His followers (John 10:10).

Reward 1

The first benefit to being a kingdom steward is answers to prayer. When we uphold our end of managing God's resources according to our commitment to Him, He responds with greater involvement in our prayer life. Psalm 50:14-15 puts it this way, "Offer to God a sacrifice of thanksgiving and pay your vows to the Most High; call upon Me in the day of trouble; I shall rescue you, and you will honor Me." When you treat God as owner while you act as manager, He is much more open to your prayer requests.

First John 3:22 couldn't state it more clearly than this: "And whatever we ask we receive from Him, because we keep His commandments and do the things that are pleasing in His sight." Please notice the dependent clause in that sentence. We are told in a straightforward manner that God answers our prayers to give us what we ask of Him when we "keep His commandments and do the things that are pleasing in His sight."

Volumes have been written on how to get your prayers answered. In bookstores, shelves are lined with books that have been dedicated solely to this subject. But 1 John 3:22 sums it up in one sentence. Manage what God has given to you according to His will and His commandments, and you will get your prayers answered. When you operate in the mindset of pleasing God with your decisions, then you can ask Him whatever you want in your prayers and He answers you. Many Christians don't get their prayers answered because they are approaching God with the wrong mindset. They are approaching God as if they are in control and as if they own their lives. When you go to God with that mindset, all you are asking Him to do is to bless you for your sake. But God desires to bless you for His sake and the good of others. He has a plan for you. He has a destiny He's designed you to live out. But in order to fulfill that destiny, you have to align your life underneath His overarching rule as you cultivate an intimate relationship with Him. Then, when you abide in Him and His will, He will give you whatever you ask for in Jesus' name.

> *When you operate in the mindset of pleasing God with your decisions, then you can ask Him whatever you want in your prayers and He answers you.*

I recall a woman some years ago who needed a car. So, she prayed for one, but in that prayer, she got rather specific. She said, "God, I want a green and blue car. Those are my two favorite colors. I don't know how to get that in a car, but it's my specific request."

After praying, she went car hunting. Not too long into her search, she found the perfect blue car. But because there was no green on it, she said, "God, I really do want blue and green in my car, but You have led me to a blue car. Please give me insight into what You are doing." I can tell you that she was not praying the prayer from the mindset of an owner. She had a steward's heart and saw everything in her life as belonging to God.

So, she spent some time debating with herself as to whether to buy the blue car or wait for her specific prayer to be answered. While she was considering her options, the salesman took her around the car, showed her everything, then lifted up the hood. Lo and behold, the motor had been painted green.

Because she held a kingdom steward's view of everything in her life, God blessed her with her specific answered prayer.

Are you approaching God as if you are in control? Do you own your life? Are you the decision-maker? When you proceed from this false assumption, you end up looking to God as though His only role in your life is to give you what you want.

In other words, when you disregard God as the owner of all that is in your life, don't expect Him to respond to your requests. But when you treat God as the owner and you become the steward, He is much more interested in the conversation. That's when you'll get a specific answer to a specific request. God is very detailed in His creative order. You can get as specific as you want with Him when you pray with a kingdom steward, God-honoring mindset.

Reward 2

The second reward you can expect as a kingdom steward is the fulfillment of God's promise to meet your need. Now, I didn't say that God promised to meet every *want*. But He did promise to meet every *need*.

Let's be clear on this: God's promise is contingent on you operating as a cheerful and generous steward. In other words, you understand that all you possess is His and should be used to bring glory to His name and to bless those serving as stewards with you in the kingdom. Philippians 4:19 reads, "And my God will supply all your needs according to His riches in glory in Christ Jesus." What people often fail to do is read the previous four verses, where Paul thanks the same people for giving abundantly to help him and others. Because they had functioned as kingdom stewards and had given to God's kingdom program, they were involved in getting the message of the gospel to people in need. They knew that life wasn't just about them but, rather, it was about being involved in impacting the lives of others.

Let's be clear on this: God's promise is contingent on you operating as a cheerful and generous steward.

Although most Christians claim Philippians 4:19 for themselves, not every Christian can rightfully claim its truth. A believer can only claim the promises inherit in verse 19 if that person is also doing what is found in verses 15-18. You can't skip verses 15-18 and jump to 19 to name it and claim it. No, you must prioritize your spiritual stewardship first. Then, when you do, God has your back. He has you covered. You are now living under His tutelage because your spiritual priorities are in order.

Gospel music artist Kirk Franklin comes over to my house regularly, just to spend time together talking and looking at Scripture. Recently he asked me why God sometimes allows our prayers not to get answered, even when we are obeying Him. There seem to be those times when God allows trials to keep coming and it doesn't look like He is meeting your needs. Those times are the exception to the rule. God does that when He is seeking to strengthen you and develop you to go to a new spiritual level. God may leave you in a season of need because He is letting you go through a trial or a wilderness experience in order to test or develop you. James 1 speaks to this more fully, and I encourage you to take some time to read that chapter. The apostle Paul experienced this on a number of occasions when God was taking him to a higher spiritual level (2 Corinthians 1:3-11; 12:7-9).

But other than those situations, when you fully live your life as a kingdom steward, God will come through for you as He has promised in Philippians 4:19.

Finally, remember that God meets your need "according to His riches in glory." Sometimes we pray for things we don't actually need. Either we fail to look at the situation honestly or we just can't see the full picture of our need for what it really is. When this happens, we find ourselves asking for things that don't actually address the real need. That's when God comes through by meeting the need rather than the request. Good stewardship always leads to God keeping His promise to meet your needs.

Reward 3

The third reward, or incentive, kingdom stewards receive is divine guidance. With all the options, opportunities, and opposition that exist in the world of work, career, investment, and business, divine guidance leads us through the plethora of these options to the best possible decision. Isaiah 48:17-18 puts it this way:

> Thus says the LORD, your Redeemer, the Holy One of Israel, "I am the LORD your God, who teaches you to profit, who leads you in the way you should go. If only you had paid attention to My commandments! Then your well-being would have been like a river, and your righteousness like the waves of the sea."

God literally says that when you pay attention to Him and let Him be the Lord your God, meaning that He is in charge, He will teach you how to profit. He will teach you how to increase what you have. God doesn't mind you making a profit. It's very biblical to legitimately grow in abundance. God expects you and me to expand what He has placed under our influence and authority. But what He really wants is for you and me to profit based on His rule and His guidance, and within the realm of His dominion over all.

When you make your decisions as a kingdom steward, He drops heaven's wisdom into your ideas. He guides you on how to experience an increase whether in your work, interests, or whatever it is you put your hand to. He shows you the way to go that will lead to increase. The way He does this is through the anointing of the Holy Spirit. What the Holy Spirit does is place the thoughts of God into your own thoughts. When you are near to God, abiding in Him and His commandments, you will have the ability to discern these thoughts and follow them. The Holy Spirit can guide you by taking the written Word of God and giving you specific illumination about how to apply the written Word to your life, your business, and your giving.

Every believer has the Holy Spirit residing within them. But not every believer has their reception to the Holy Spirit's guidance turned on. Yet when it is turned on, you will be guided by God Himself on how to profit.

The famed financial advisor Dave Ramsey shares in his testimony about how he was making a lot of money in his midtwenties but was also in a lot of debt.[1] He tells how he had several degrees in financial planning after his name but all they spelled (in his words) was "dumb," because he was obviously not profiting off of his increase as he sank further and further in debt. When asked what caused the turnaround in his own financial life, Ramsey points to Proverbs. In that one book, he says, God has all we need to know on how to manage our money. When he started making all financial decisions based on that one book, things changed.

This is a perfect example of the Holy Spirit's ability to take God's Word and guide you on how to steward the resources He's given to you. The entirety of the Bible gives guidance, and when you discover the power of the Spirit to enlighten you, you will make decisions that lead to good rather than to ruin.

God really wants to guide you. His anointing has been given so that we might navigate our way through the difficulties of life, moving with a divine purpose and avoiding any pitfalls. Don't let the wandering of your life cause you to lose hope. If you commit to following Him, letting Him be Lord and Master of all, you will find that your wanderings turn into a purposeful direction. But that comes about only when you commit to obeying Him in every area of your life.

The Bible is replete with stories where God's people failed to remember that God was their Lord, worthy of their allegiance and obedience. Those failures led to wandering, suffering, and punishment. The same Bible is also full of stories where God's people repented, got it right, and followed Him without condition. That led to redemption, prosperity, and divine guidance.

> *If you commit to following Him, letting Him be Lord and Master of all, you will find that your wanderings turn into a purposeful direction.*

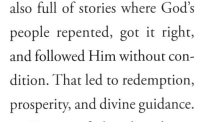

You may feel as though you are wandering around in the desert, lost and in need of direction. The good news is that it doesn't have to be that way. You have been given the Holy Spirit, whereby you can benefit from everlasting direction and protection. Think of Him as a signal caller, who places ideas and thoughts in your mind. Now, sure, those thoughts and ideas may not always seem to make sense, but if you obey Him, He can turn your situation around.

Remember the account from 1 Kings 17 about the widow who was down to her last meal? As far as she knew, she and her son were going to eat their last meal and then they would die shortly thereafter. But God sent the prophet Elijah to her and said to tell her that she was to feed him with what she had left. In Old Testament times, God spoke through prophets. Today He speaks through the Holy Spirit consistent with His written Word. Because the woman listened to the guidance and command of God through the prophet and fed Elijah in faith with all she had left, God prospered her. He provided more than enough for her to feed herself and her son from that time forward.

God's guidance doesn't always make sense but it does make miracles. When you choose to operate under what God says and in accordance with His will as a kingdom steward, even (or especially) when it doesn't make sense, you can rest assured that He will steer you in the path of His provision.

Reward 4

The fourth reward God offers you as a kingdom steward is that of living a purpose-filled life instead of an empty one. Every believer has been given pre-ordained good works to perform for God's glory and the advancement of His kingdom during their earthly pilgrimage (Ephesians 2:10). A good work is a divinely ordained task that honors God and impacts people physically, socially, and spiritually (Acts 13:36). We must prioritize the kingdom assignments we were created and saved to accomplish. Now, keep in mind, a satisfied and purpose-filled life does not necessarily consist of an abundance of

The moment abundance becomes your primary goal, life begins to ebb from you because a person's life does not consist of the abundance of stuff he possesses.

possessions. In fact, it is common to possess much and still have nothing. People can have a large house but find little satisfaction living there. They can buy a new car but remain unhappy with where they are going. Life has to do with finding the purpose for living. It is found when a person embraces a spiritual pursuit over just a material one.

The moment abundance becomes your primary goal, life begins to ebb from you because a person's life does not consist of the abundance of stuff he possesses (Luke 12:15). If you think you are an owner of something, let me use this moment to call you into the reality of eternity. A lot of us are waiting for a retirement that we may never see. If you're waiting for your Social Security income to kick in at age sixty-five before you start living, what happens if you leave this earth at sixty-four? Start living your life now by pursuing the purpose that the Owner has given to you. With a kingdom perspective, you can enjoy purpose-filled living instead of pursuing pointless possessions.

In Luke 12:15-21, Jesus gives us insight into the emptiness that comes when a person fails to access this reward of a purpose-filled life. We read,

> Then He said to them, "Beware, and be on your guard against
> every form of greed; for not even when one has an abundance does
> his life consist of his possessions." And He told them a parable,
> saying, "The land of a rich man was very productive. And he began
> reasoning to himself, saying, 'What shall I do, since I have no place
> to store my crops?' Then he said, 'This is what I will do: I will
> tear down my barns and build larger ones, and there I will store
> all my grain and my goods. And I will say to my soul, "Soul, you
> have many goods laid up for many years to come; take your ease,
> eat, drink and be merry."' But God said to him, 'You fool! This
> very night your soul is required of you; and now who will own
> what you have prepared?' So is the man who stores up treasure for
> himself, and is not rich toward God."

When you confuse ownership with management, you will place the emphasis of your investments in the wrong location. There is nothing wrong with the legitimate accumulation and enjoyment of things. But the minute you make that your life's definition and reason for being, you are losing the very life you sought to save. It doesn't matter how much money is in your bank account if your spiritual account is at zero. Existing is not the same as living. Having stuff doesn't automatically make you good at life, just as having kids doesn't automatically make you good at being a parent.

Meaning comes from alignment under God and fulfilling His kingdom purposes.

What we have done in our world today is switch the priorities. We have made stuff the defining element of meaning because we have bought into the devil's lies. Life does not consist of things. Meaning comes from alignment under God and fulfilling His kingdom purposes.

Reward 5

The fifth reward kingdom stewards receive is emotional stability. Stress and worry cripple millions every day. We worry about money, health, family, crime, and a myriad of other things. It's like the man who said he'd give $1000 to anyone who would do his worrying for him. When a man volunteered and then asked for his money, the man replied, "Well, that's the first thing you need to worry about."

We find so much to fear in this world, and the enemy loves nothing more than to see God's precious children living panic-stricken lives. It comes in different shapes and sizes. Depression, frustration, anger, violence—all these emotions show up, and in response to them, we medicate ourselves to death. In the middle of all this, God has the audacity to say, "Don't worry."

What is worry, anyway? It's more than concern; it's concern gone haywire. It's like a rocking chair; it'll get you started, but it ultimately won't take you anywhere. Friend, worry is one of the most blatant sins because worry is doubting the power and goodness of God. Some people don't

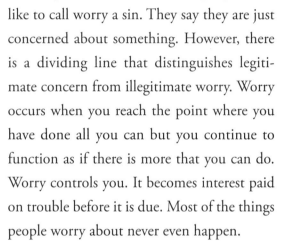

To worry about your life is to forget who your Father is. He provides for all creation, including you.

like to call worry a sin. They say they are just concerned about something. However, there is a dividing line that distinguishes legitimate concern from illegitimate worry. Worry occurs when you reach the point where you have done all you can but you continue to function as if there is more that you can do. Worry controls you. It becomes interest paid on trouble before it is due. Most of the things people worry about never even happen.

The real problem for most people is how to stop worrying in difficult situations. When the rent is due, the bank account is empty, and the family needs to be fed, worry can become an all-consuming state of mind. In Luke 12:28, Jesus says to His disciples, "You men of little faith!" The point He is making is that worry is evidence of a faith problem. To worry about your life is to forget who your Father is. He provides for all creation, including you. It might seem like He's asleep in the boat, but in reality, He wants you to trust Him and take rest in His abundant provision.

When I was growing up in Baltimore, my dad was a longshoreman and sometimes there would be a gap in his work assignments. He would look for other ways to make money in order to provide for the family. But sometimes there wouldn't be enough money left over for food. In those times, my dad would go fishing. He would catch enough herring to feed the entire family for breakfast, lunch, dinner, and dessert. In fact, we ate so much herring that I can't bear to eat fish anymore as an adult.

Even though I may not have cared for the taste of herring, I never went to bed hungry. What's more, I never went to bed worrying if there would be enough to eat. That's because I knew my dad would provide.

What God wants us to remember is that when we live our lives according to His spiritual principles, we do not have to worry. He is our faithful Father and He will supply. If my human daddy can make a way out of nowhere to feed his family, what do you think our Heavenly Father can do? You and I just need to live in sync with His will and His ownership to experience His covering. When we do, we will see the hand of God actively involved in our lives. In fact, God is so good at taking care of things that He doesn't even need our help for everything He does. Psalm 127:2 says, "It is vain for you to rise up early, to retire late, to eat the bread of painful labors; for He gives to His beloved even in his sleep."

While you are sleeping, God is planning. While you are sleeping, God is working things out. God never sleeps and He never slumbers. What's more, God never leaves His righteous forsaken (Psalm 37:25). I don't know how God will solve your problem or fix your concerns but I can guarantee you that if you commit to living your life fully as a kingdom steward, managing all He's given to you according to His principles, He will take care of you. You do not need to worry. What you need to do is seek Him, obey Him, and then rest in the promise of His care. As Jeremiah 17:7-8 teaches, God will even care for His people in a drought.

Reward 6

The sixth reward you can tap into when living as a kingdom steward is experiencing divine reversals where God turns things around in your life for the better. In Malachi 3:11, we read, "'Then I will rebuke the devourer for you, so that it will not destroy the fruits of the ground; nor will your vine in the field cast its grapes,' says the LORD of hosts." The devourer is someone who seeks to rip off your blessing from you. They want to eat up your produce. Satan is the foremost devourer, and he uses people and situations to go about his plan.

But we are told of God's response to the devourer in John 10:10 when Jesus says, "The thief comes only to steal and kill and destroy; I came that they may have life, and have it abundantly." When Jesus is positioned as Lord of your life, God can introduce a divine reversal of Satan's plan of attack. But far too often we fail to position ourselves rightly. You see, stewardship is all about positioning yourself under God's overarching rule in your life. Most people think stewardship has to do merely with how a person manages his or her money. While that is an important aspect of stewardship, it is only one aspect. Living as a kingdom steward is an all-inclusive awareness and perspective that all you have been given by God is His to use for His glory. Your time, your talents, and your treasures belong to Him. Yet because we fail to realize this and take it into account, Satan continues to rip us off. There are so many believers who are living lives of loss due to what the enemy has stolen. Maybe you are one of them. He has stolen some of your talents or your resources. It could be that he has stolen your hope, dreams, or even your time. Satan may have ripped away years from you that had been meant by God for good but wound up being wasted. Perhaps he has twisted your thinking to such a degree that now you are living in perpetual debt and slavery to the almighty dollar, just trying to break even. Satan seeks to rip you off, whether through stealing your peace or provisions.

Whatever he may have stolen from you, if you will discover the secret of right alignment in God's all-encompassing will—you will see God turn things around. You will witness a reversal of fortune when God rebukes the devourer and commands him to leave you alone.

I remember the black-and-white *Superman* television show that I would watch frequently as a young kid. In one episode, the *Daily Planet* is on fire, and Superman flies in and saves a man just before the building collapses. They fly high into the sky, and as you might expect, the man is terrified. Superman has flown so high, he and the man are practically in outer space. So the man starts panicking. Then Superman looks at this frightened man and says, "What makes you think that having delivered you from the fire, I would drop you now?"

That's often how it is with us and God. We have been delivered from the fires of hell. What makes us think that He would allow us to fall while here on earth? The real problem is one of positioning. We don't position ourselves right with God, and we leave ourselves exposed to the enemy and his plans to devour us.

Yes, Satan comes to steal, kill, and destroy. What's worse is that we let him because we leave ourselves exposed. We invite him to eat our blessing, steal our talent, or rob us of our reward. But God wants us to remember that as the Owner, He's got us. He's not going to drop us. Therefore, we need to renew our belief that no matter the circumstances, we need to stay in alignment with our Owner and not leave ourselves exposed to the enemy. This reversal of fortune from calamity to salvation should fill us with great hope and faith in Him.

> *We have been delivered from the fires of hell. What makes us think that He would allow us to fall while here on earth?*

Reward 7

The seventh reward you can anticipate receiving when you live as a kingdom steward is the opportunity to co-reign with Christ in His coming millennial kingdom. There is a lot of misconception about heaven. You're not going to be sitting on a cloud playing your harp. Heaven is civilization.

Scripture talks about cities. Jesus talks about ruling. Earth is the only known civilization, but when God re-creates the heavens and the earth and the whole universe can now be expanded, it will go beyond that. We know it includes earth, but it also reaches beyond that. The Bible promises different levels of rewards in this future kingdom based on your stewardship on earth.

You need to understand that going to heaven and not being able to experience an abundance of heavenly rewards will be a reality to many people. One of these rewards is an ability to govern, or co-reign, with Christ in an area of authority. In the parable of the master and his three servants in Luke 19, the first two servants are promised authority over a number of cities in accordance with their good stewardship with what they had been given. However, the third servant received a rebuke. The point is that "co-reigning" with Christ comes as a reward for those who live as faithful stewards of His kingdom. It is not a guarantee for everyone who enters heaven. The level of your ability to govern, whether it be over a block, one city, two cities, or whatever region you are given, will come as a direct correlation to how well you stewarded the time, talents, and treasures God gave you while on earth. So don't settle for being a street sweeper in Christ's coming kingdom because you refuse to function as a kingdom steward in this life. Live this life in light of the life that is to come. Remember that the more you have been given, the more God is expecting from you in expanding His kingdom and bringing Him greater glory (Luke 12:48).

11

*

RELEASE

We have finally come to the topic of debt. As a reminder, a kingdom steward is a believer who faithfully oversees the protection and expansion of the assets God has entrusted to him or her to manage on His behalf. All of what you have is to fall underneath God's overarching rule. Now, that also involves our responsibility to properly manage our money.

Money is a major issue with God in Scripture. In eleven of Jesus' thirty-nine parables, He addresses various issues related to money. These include investing (Matthew 13:44-46), saving (Matthew 13:52), debt (Matthew 18:23-35), wage structures (Matthew 20:1-16), leasing (Matthew 21:33-41), banking (Matthew 25:14-30), debt cancellation (Luke 7:41-43), accumulating resources (Luke 12:16-21), cost analysis (Luke 14:28-30), and estate planning (Luke 15:11-32). It serves as an indicator light that reveals the true nature of our hearts.

One of the beautiful bounties and benefits of being a kingdom steward is that the Owner takes ultimate responsibility for his management team. When you insist on acting as an owner rather than as a manager, you will have to take responsibility for the outcomes yourself. Self-ownership creates a major problem in our culture because it places these so-called owners at the mercy of their own control. As a result, far too many believers are drowning in a sea of debt—unable to live their lives as God designed them to be lived, while others find themselves enslaved to the god of their wealth, making them enemies of the true God. You cannot worship God and money (Matthew 6:24). Rather, we are to use money to draw our hearts in a Godward direction (Matthew 6:19-24).

—— ✿ ——

One of the beautiful bounties and benefits of being a kingdom steward is that the Owner takes ultimate responsibility for his management team.

—— ✿ ——

There is a reward to your kingdom stewardship and that is the reward of financial freedom. God wants you to be free from slavery to illegitimate debt. Slavery may be a harsh-sounding term but it's an accurate, biblical term. As Proverbs 22:7 says, "The rich rules over the poor, and the borrower becomes the lender's slave." Illegitimate debt has become an addiction for far too many people. They find themselves financially strapped day in and day out—year after year and decade after decade. Borrowing and servitude go hand in hand.

Living lives trapped under the weight of never-ending debt can lead to depression, family conflict, worry, and many more emotional difficulties that can entice people, even believers, to other forms of bondage in efforts to cope. Stewarding your money wisely is an issue far greater than good money management. It is an issue of overall well-being and freedom. Wise stewardship ushers in the reward of financial capacity for enjoyment, investment, and rest.

Yet, unfortunately, some of us need to change the name of our Visa cards to Voluntary Institutional Slavery Always because we are owned by the repayment of our debt. We make minimum payments that go on forever, dictating our decisions and limiting our freedom of choice. Instead of living for the future, we wind up paying for the past, causing us to live mortgaged lives. For far too many, their theme song is "I owe, I owe, so off to work I go." We live in a world of the haves and the have-nots, but for most people, it is the have-not-paid-for what they have. This principle applies to people on every level of the economic spectrum since even the rich can over-leverage themselves and their businesses.

God says that living according to His principles means living with the reward of being debt-free, which means not creating bills that you are unable to pay. He tells us in Deuteronomy 28:12, "The LORD will open for you His good storehouse, the heavens, to give rain to your land in its season and to bless all the work of your hand; and you shall lend to many nations, but you shall not borrow." According to this passage, you are to be the lender, not the borrower. That is to be the case for those who follow God and His rule over their lives. This makes the issue of debt a spiritual one. It is more than a human addiction. It is a spiritual stronghold that must be addressed spiritually.

But the Lord also gives us insight into what happens when we do not live our lives according to His principles. When we choose through our choices not to follow Him, we will wind up in perpetual debt. Deuteronomy 28:43-44 says, "The alien who is among you shall rise above you higher and higher, but

Disobedience to God leads to illegitimate debt.

you will go down lower and lower. He shall lend to you, but you will not lend to him; he shall be the head, and you will be the tail."

Disobedience to God leads to illegitimate debt. Now, by debt I am not talking about simply having bills. We all pay recurring bills for things such as electricity, a house, or a car. When the Bible talks about illegitimate debt, it's referencing bills you cannot pay, or money owed that you are unable to pay in a timely manner, or where your liabilities exceed your assets, or where you are out of alignment with your financial priorities because of inappropriate financial obligations. God does not want that type of living to be normal for believers. He even told the Israelites in Deuteronomy 15:1-2,

> At the end of every seven years you shall grant a remission of debts. This is the manner of remission: every creditor shall release what he has loaned to his neighbor; he shall not exact it of his neighbor and his brother, because the LORD's remission has been proclaimed.

In essence, He instructed His people never to hold debt against someone else for longer than seven years. God knows the importance of personal freedom and what is needed for expansion. He never intended for His followers to experience a lifetime of economic slavery. We no longer live under the law of jubilee or the automatic remission of debts every seven years, but we still are to apply biblical principles to our finances in order to be set free from debt.

There are four primary reasons in our Christian culture today why so many people find themselves in long-term, unrighteous consumer debt. These include spiritual ignorance of God's principles on money, overspending, poor planning, and bad preaching/teaching on this subject.

Thankfully, there are also four things you can do to get out of the prison of illegitimate consumer debt and toward the experience of the reward of financial freedom. These include planting, planning, prioritizing, and praying.

Plant, Plan, Prioritize, and Pray

For starters, planting involves investing what you do have in God's kingdom. It means giving to God first. When I was in Israel recently, my family and I took some time to visit a re-created town of Nazareth. It was one of the highlights of the trip. They made this town look like it would have during the time Jesus walked on earth. One of the fascinating places in the town was a small room where they demonstrated to us how they made olive oil in Bible times. They had a donkey pulling a millstone around in a circle. This 1,000-pound stone would grind the olives that had been placed in the basin, and it would cause the olives to crack. We could literally hear the olives cracking. Once they cracked open, the oil would flow out of the olive.

The first batch of oil is the best. The Israelites set this oil aside as an offering to God. Then, after the first batch was collected, they would add another weighted stone to bring out the second batch of oil. This second batch of oil was used to run the house. It was for cooking and cleaning. The third time the stone would crush the olives, it produced the last batch, which would be used for lighting lamps.

In other words, everything was done intentionally in an order that recognized God as the source. The best oil was given to God in an offering. The second-best oil was used for consumption and everyday living needs. The final oil allowed for the luxury of light. Light wasn't essential to living but it provided additional opportunities for a person through the expansion of the day, either for productivity or enjoyment.

God believes in planning. God Himself is a planner.

Friend, if you have a need—are you willing to plant a seed? Planting involves investing first and foremost in God's kingdom purposes, which establishes Him as your source (Deuteronomy 14:23).

Second, you must establish a short- and long-term plan. Proverbs 27:23 gives great biblical wisdom, "Know well the condition of your flocks, and pay attention to your herds." This one verse establishes a basic business and financial principle for all of us: Stop guessing. Know how many sheep you have, and how well they are doing. Do the hard work of assessment, understanding, learning, and application as it relates to whatever revenue-producing ventures you take part in. You must have a plan. And in order to have a plan, you must clearly comprehend the marketplace, your assets, and the strategies for increase.

God believes in planning. God Himself is a planner. He planned things out before the foundation of the world (Ephesians 1:4). Yet far too many of us will go to Him without doing the diligence of planning ourselves. In essence, we are asking Him to bless our nothingness. We send up vague prayers for vague needs only to get vague answers because we do not believe in the specificity of how God works. God works in concert and in cadence with plans. You regularly witness Him in Scripture responding to a plan, tweaking a plan, or creating a plan.

A financial plan starts with a budget. Everyone should be living according to a budget. This gives you the framework within which you are seeking to remove debt and free up spending for all your needs, as well as greater giving to God's kingdom. A budget enables you to live within your means. Proverbs 21:5 makes it clear that planning is essential for prospering: "The plans of the diligent lead surely to advantage, but everyone who is hasty comes surely to poverty." You must plan. Don't operate in the mindset of luck or undefined hope. Far too many people try to luck themselves into a solution. But God says time and time again in His Word that He's given you a mind in order to plan. Diligence ushers in growth. A hasty pursuit after wealth, whether that be through gambling, the lottery, or any other similar means, is spoken about clearly in God's Word. We read:

There is precious treasure and oil in the dwelling of the wise, but a foolish man swallows it up.

PROVERBS 21:20

Prepare your work outside and make it ready for yourself in the field; afterwards, then, build your house.

PROVERBS 24:27

He who tills his land will have plenty of food, but he who follows
empty pursuits will have poverty in plenty.

PROVERBS 28:19

A faithful man will abound with blessings, but he who makes
haste to be rich will not go unpunished.

PROVERBS 28:20

A man with an evil eye hastens after wealth and does not know
that want will come upon him.

PROVERBS 28:22

No wise person spends everything they get. God responds to the effective and strategic use of the wealth He has given to you. This comes about
through careful planning. Godly financial
planners can assist you in this regard as well,
especially when it comes to setting long-term
goals, which also should include making a will,
having adequate insurance, saving for college
and retirement, etc. A basic beginning budget
might look similar to this: 10 percent giving,
10 percent short-term savings, 10 percent debt

> *No wise person
> spends every-
> thing they get.*

reduction, 60 percent living expenses, 5 percent long-term savings, 5 percent cushion. Proverbs 15:22 says, "Without consultation, plans are frus-
trated, but with many counselors they succeed."

Third, you must prioritize financial freedom. One of the ways you
prioritize financial freedom and getting out of debt is through discern-
ing between wants and needs. We have looked at this in detail during the
chapter on contentment, so I'll only mention it briefly here. Far too many
people are confused between their wants and their needs. Having a car is a
"need" in most places in today's culture. Having a souped-up, brand-new,

leather-interior car is a "want." To start the process toward financial freedom involves identifying any wants that you have falsely treated as needs. Once you do, you can begin to redirect your resources toward the removal of any excess debt.

I remember my son Jonathan came to me when he was younger and just starting to play sports. He told me that he needed a brand-new pair of Air Jordans. Now, if you know anything about Air Jordans, you probably know they are over-priced. I had to explain to Jonathan that he had confused his needs with his wants. He "wanted" a new pair of Air Jordans. All he really "needed" was a pair of tennis shoes. I offered to pay the price of the tennis shoes and then if he wanted the Air Jordans instead, he could work to pay the difference.

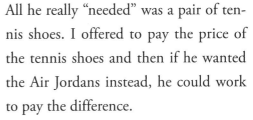

> *God has promised to meet the needs of faithful, generous believers, not necessarily their wants.*

God has promised to meet the needs of faithful, generous believers, not necessarily their wants (Philippians 4:15-19). Rather than live a life of complaining about all that you don't have, reclassify what you don't have in the proper category of "wants," and replace the ingratitude with gratitude. This will give you better perspective for prioritizing where your money goes. Once you do that, you can focus on paying your smallest bills first. After you pay off your smallest bill, focus on paying off your next smallest bill. Utilizing the additional dollars from the previous paid-off bills, continue doing that until you have removed all illegitimate consumer debt.

Prioritizing the paying off of your debt also helps to curb impulse purchases. Once you commit to where your money goes, you will be less likely to spend impulsively.

Fourth, you are to pray. I didn't place prayer last because it's the least important. I placed prayer last because after you do the first three things, you now know what to pray for. You will be able to talk to God in your prayers very specifically because you have planted, planned, and prioritized your financial resources.

God is a debt-canceling God and He will never forsake you (Hebrews 13:5). But His promises come under the covering of His covenant. Unless you align yourself underneath His rightful rule in your life as a kingdom steward, you cannot tap into the promises of His provision. God seeks to set people free. In fact, He has very interesting ways of doing it. In Proverbs 13:22 we read, "The wealth of the sinner is stored up for the righteous." God will even use the wealth of others to turn your situation around. That's why you cannot predict Him. You can never know exactly what He is up to.

God has all kinds of ways to accomplish His will. He is not bound by human logic or reasoning. But you will never gain access into His powerful provision if you choose to function according to your own wisdom rather than His. As you align the use of your time, talents, and treasures underneath His overarching rule, you will witness the supernatural invade the natural. That's what the Bible calls being truly rich, when you get to see heaven join you on earth and absolutely blow your mind.

Give, Save, Spend

Once you have established the foundation of financial accountability through the four principles of planting, planning, prioritizing, and praying, you are able to wisely handle your money according to these next three steps. They are: give, save, and spend.

If you will begin to fully apply these three words, in this order, to your financial choices, you will begin to see your financial life be immensely rewarded. Your path to financial freedom is completely tied to these three words.

I have touched on the concept of giving in an earlier chapter. Unless and until you get this part of your financial stewardship right, you will not experience the fullness of the financial blessings that God has in store for you. This principle is the foundation upon which all else is built since it establishes your recognition of God as your Source.

Unfortunately, in Christian circles today we are experiencing a condition that I call Cirrhosis of the Giver. It is estimated that less than 20 percent of all Christians faithfully tithe. And we wonder why we are experiencing financial struggles, strain, and defeat. When we fail to live out God's principles with regard to stewardship, and in particular giving, we fail to reap God's blessings with regard to reward and provision. We also leave the church short of the kingdom resources necessary to have the kingdom impact God expects His people to make in the world. You can't be a kingdom steward and a spiritual thief at the same time and simultaneously expect the blessings of God.

The reward of financial freedom involves honoring God with your finances. If you skip that basic premise, it won't matter what else you do. God has scissors and your pockets will have holes (Haggai 1:6). I was twenty-two years old when I learned this principle. At the time, all I made was $350 a month. We weren't just poor, we were "po!" Yet even though all I made was $350 a month, before we did anything else at all, a tithe of $35 was given to God as well as an offering of $15. In giving the tithe and offering to God, I wasn't just telling Him that I was giving Him my money. I was telling Him that I knew that He is the owner and I am the steward and that all I have is His.

It is such a simple principle that it amazes me how many people don't believe it, operate by it, or benefit from it. God didn't make the road to financial victory a mystery. He set up a signpost, clearly marked, and said, "Give to Me, then I will protect you, provide for you, and promote what you do."

Yet so many people say, "Tony, I can't afford to tithe." To which I reply, "You can't afford not to." You need all the help you can get, and that help comes from God. Don't rob God and then expect to experience all that He wishes to bless you with. You are ripping off the One who has the power to help you.

Another question I often hear with regard to the tithe is, "Tony, does God want me to tithe off of the gross or off of the net?" To which I reply, "Do you want God to bless the gross or the net?" It's your call. God has made it clear what the solution is. He hasn't hidden the answer. It's up to you whether or not you follow. It's up to you whether or not you position yourself to receive the rewards, or position yourself to live life carrying bags or purses with holes in them.

The second step on the path to experiencing the reward of financial freedom involves an equally unfamiliar word in many circles today: save. Savings is the opposite of debt because savings is future-oriented while illegitimate consumer debt, as opposed to wise investments, is past-oriented. Savings involve putting away something for tomorrow while debt involves paying for yesterday. Unfortunately, around 40 percent of Americans do not have enough savings to cover a $400 emergency.[1]

Savings is the opposite of debt because savings is future-oriented while illegitimate consumer debt, as opposed to wise investments, is past-oriented.

In fact, biblical principles on money include not only saving for yourself but also saving for your descendants. Proverbs 13:22 says, "A good man leaves an inheritance to his children's children." You aren't merely to be thinking of yourself with regard to your financial plans, you are to be making plans for your grandchildren as well.

Yet most Christians today can't even get around to the grandchildren because they haven't gotten around to the children, and worse yet, they haven't gotten around to saving for themselves. The majority of believers are one crisis away from bankruptcy.

The greatest biblical illustration of the benefits of saving comes from the life of Joseph. The principles that Joseph followed while in Egypt not only blessed him, but they also blessed his family and entire nations. Pharaoh had a dream that he could not understand, which included seven fat cows and seven lean cows as well as seven good ears of corn and seven scorched ears of corn. Joseph's God-given interpretation of that dream gives us one of the greatest precepts for financial victory we could ever follow. Joseph instructed Pharaoh to take from the abundance of the harvest and save it so that when the time came for Egypt and the surrounding nations to experience lack, they would have a surplus to fall back on. Scripture tells us Joseph's instructions,

> Let Pharaoh take action to appoint overseers in charge of the land, and let him exact a fifth of the produce of the land of Egypt in the seven years of abundance. Then let them gather all the food of these good years that are coming, and store up the grain for food in the cities under Pharaoh's authority, and let them guard it. Let the food become as a reserve for the land for the seven years of famine which will occur in the land of Egypt, so that the land will not perish during the famine.
>
> GENESIS 41:34-36

Joseph advised Pharaoh to set aside and save during the years of plenty so that there would be enough to supply everyone's needs in the years of famine. You never know when you are going to run into a month, year, or even a decade of famine. Many people were caught off guard when our nation's economy took a downturn in 2008. This is because they had not learned the principle of living a life of financial victory that includes saving for the future.

Both tithing and saving should be so automatic that you take off of the top of your earnings with no questions asked. Even if you have to start out saving only a small amount, you still need to do it. You need to develop the habit of saving. Cultivate the virtue of saying no to instant gratification and yes to prolonged stability.

Parents should also be teaching their children how to save. An early and steady habit of saving will yield big rewards in the long term. They should be taught to consistently put away a percentage of their income and seek to grow that percentage as their age and income expands. This will establish savings as a lifestyle.

Cultivate the virtue of saying no to instant gratification and yes to prolonged stability.

Yet because we as parents fail to model a healthy and biblical worldview of savings to our children, we see them spend, spend, spend rather than save, save, save. It is a fool who spends everything he has. If I told you that you were going to die, yet there was a $5,000 surgery that could save your life but your insurance doesn't cover it, would you find that money somehow? Most likely, you would. You would discover a way to come up with $5,000. This is because saving this money has now become a priority to you. We make the things happen in our lives that are a priority for us. Your future should be a priority for you.

God illustrates this through one of the smallest creatures on earth, whose wisdom concerning saving is much greater than that of most of us. We read, "Go to the ant, O sluggard, observe her ways and be wise, which, having no chief, officer or ruler, prepares her food in the summer and gathers her provision in the harvest" (Proverbs 6:6-8). The ant knows how to gather and store away for later; however, many people today who hold bachelor's, master's, or even higher degrees have not yet learned this principle. And then we wonder why there is so much stress when it comes to the handling of finances.

Many of us are not saving money because we have maxed out our personal budgets already. We don't see any surplus to set aside for later because every dollar that comes in is already claimed for something. Our house note, car note, grocery bill, and entertainment bill along with student loans and everything else use up all that we earn. However, there are a few practical tips that you can do to cut back on your expenses in an effort to save money. While these do not include all the money-saving tips that can put you in a better position to save, these are what I call my top ten tips to reduce expenses and manage your money so that you can become a better, wiser kingdom steward:

1. After giving and saving, pay off your debt starting with the smallest bill first. A lot of money these days is going to pay interest on credit cards, thus making it difficult for people to save. I know it is easier said than done, but there are several strategies for paying credit card debt. The first involves checking with your lenders and asking if they can give you a lower interest rate if you close the account and work toward paying the balance. Another way is to consolidate your credit card debt into one loan that gives you a lower interest rate. Credit card interest rates can run upwards of 20 to 30 percent. A lower interest rate will allow more of your monthly payment to go to principle and less to interest. Just be careful that you either close your account or do not add more debt to your credit cards. Most importantly, stop borrowing from credit cards to pay bills. Do plastic surgery, if necessary, by cutting up your credit cards and operating on cash.

2. Cut back on entertainment costs. People do not need to spend so much money each month on a large cable subscription, particularly

with the invention of cheap or even free ways to view entertainment through Hulu.com, Netflix, and other services. A lot of what you want to view these days can be accessed through the Internet, inexpensive rentals, or the library. In addition, wisely choose when you go to the movies. Matinees may offer you the same viewing experience for less than an evening show. Don't blow your savings on overpriced popcorn or soda. Eat before you go so you won't be tempted to buy.

3. Use cash. Rarely these days do you see anyone paying with cash. However, using cash as your primary method of payment gives you a way of seeing how much you really have. Once you have a budget, consider how much you have allocated for food, gas, or anything else that you plan to buy and set aside the cash for those purchases. This way you will have a more accurate understanding of how much you have to spend, and you will be unable to spend more than you budgeted. When the cash is gone for the month, so is the spending. It will only take one or two months of running out early for you to learn principles of spending that will help you to not run out in the future.

4. Pay off your car or your home early. You can save a tremendous amount of money simply by making additional payments that are applied strictly to the principal. Once your car or home is paid off, use the extra money to invest in your future. Also consider alternating car purchases so that when one car is paid off, you keep putting away the same note amount until you have another to buy the next car for cash.

5. In addition to paying off your car, choose your car wisely. Choosing a car that conserves gas rather than wastes it is an optimal choice. Yet whatever car you drive can use less gas simply by how you drive

it. Using cruise control while on the highways as well as accelerating slowly rather than quickly can economize the use of fuel.

6. Install energy-saving lightbulbs throughout your home. It has been shown that replacing high-energy bulbs with compact fluorescent lights can trim your electrical bill by nearly 25 percent.

7. Cook at home and eat leftovers. Americans spend roughly a little over one-third of their annual food budget on eating out. Not only is eating out frequently a poor choice for your health because of the abundance of processed food, it is also a poor choice for your wallet if you are battling debt. Consider spending more time planning your grocery list, grocery shopping, cooking, and also eating leftovers. Be sure to shop when you are not hungry. Use the extra money that you save on your monthly food bill for savings or paying down your debt.

8. Develop short-term savings of three to six months to meet essential living expenses in an emergency, and develop long-term savings to address retirement and legacy.

9. Shop around to make sure that you have the absolutely lowest insurance premium on your home, car, and health insurance that gives you the best possible coverage. Insurance companies are competitive and will often beat another company's price simply to get your business. Do your due diligence on insurance and invest the money you save.

10. Lose weight God's way. Americans spend over $20 billion annually on weight loss products, equipment, memberships, and surgeries.[2] It is one of the top moneymakers in existence. And yet we wouldn't need to lose weight if we followed the biblical principles of taking care of our bodies as the temple of the Holy Spirit, by not giving into behaviors of greed, excess, and gluttony. The basics of losing weight

typically involve self-control and discipline. Limit simple carbohydrates and sugar intake while balancing your diet with healthy complex carbs, proteins, and fats. A healthy diet along with consistent exercise doesn't cost much and will produce steady and long-term results. Walking outside for thirty minutes is free. Driving to a nearby park only costs gas. Either set up a membership at a local gym or set up an at-home exercise gym. Look for used equipment instead of buying new. Many people have bought at-home exercise equipment only to find they do not use it. These people are often willing to sell their equipment at greatly reduced prices.

There are multiple strategies you can employ to cut back on your expenses in an effort to redirect those funds either to paying down your debt or to saving. These are just a few. Yet whatever you do, begin the process of saving now. Even if it's just to get you used to the concept until you are able to save a larger portion of your income each month, start now. At a minimum, you should aim to have three to four months of living expenses in a savings account. Money above that should be used for investment opportunities or retirement funds.

Financial wisdom comes from making your highest priority fearing God and honoring Him with how you use the money He gives you to steward for Him.

God has given you a way to enjoy the rewards of material blessings from His hand, but not apart from following His principles and wisdom. Financial freedom comes through financial wisdom. Financial wisdom comes from making your highest priority fearing God and honoring Him with how you use the money He gives you to steward for Him.

The third area that you should focus on regarding your finances is how you spend. Once you have given to God, and once you have saved a portion of your money, the remainder of what you have is yours to spend. But don't go spend it on anything and everything. The Bible has principles related to your spending habits as well. The first one I want to touch on again briefly is your budget. You need a budget. Without a budget, you will not be able to make the most of your money, and you will run the risk of spending more than you have. As we saw earlier in this chapter, God is in the planning business. He wants to bless a plan.

If a blessing stops with you, it is incomplete. God blesses in order for you to bless. Plan to bless.

We read in Proverbs, "Commit your works to the LORD and your plans will be established" (Proverbs 16:3). I am amazed at the number of families whom I counsel who do not have a financial plan. Every Christian family should have a plan for how they expect to spend the resources God has given them. If there is no plan, then there is nothing to ask God to help out with.

If you do not have a financial plan for where your money will go when it comes in with each paycheck, you need to make one now. If you already have one, make sure it lines up with the following principles, because if you will practice and live by these precepts, you will live in financial victory. That is not to say you will be a millionaire but it is to say that you will have the capacity to enjoy and maximize the financial blessings and resources God has given you in your life.

As we looked at earlier, make sure that your needs come before your wants, or you may end up losing your needs at the expense of your wants. And leave room in your budget for helping others. The greatest command is to love God with all of your heart. The second greatest command is to love others. If God has blessed you with financial gain in any way, it is so He can use it to be a blessing to others as well. The definition of a blessing is being able to enjoy and extend the favor of God in your life. If a blessing stops with you, it is incomplete. God blesses in order for you to bless. Plan to be a blessing. You will be amazed at how great it feels to be able to assist someone in need. We read in Acts,

> In everything I showed you that by working hard in this manner you must help the weak and remember the words of the Lord Jesus, that He Himself said, "It is more blessed to give than to receive."
>
> ACTS 20:35

Invest in others with the resources that God has given you, and you will be blessed (Proverbs 11:24-27). It is a guarantee. Give, save, learn how to be content with what you have, use your money wisely, plan a budget for what you receive, and you will be walking on the path to financial victory.

Remember, there is nothing wrong with having things unless you can't pay your bills and the money that God has given you is going to interest on accumulated debt. That is when it is time to see what you can sell in order to pay what you owe. You must make the decision now to start living within your means, avoiding unnecessary borrowing and developing a short- and long-term financial plan. Give God something specific to respond to.

But what I can tell you is that if you will put Him and His principles first in your life, He will show you His plan for you.

Friend, God has a plan for you. If you are struggling with debt today and you take the time and the effort to seek Him, He has a plan to bring you to the reward of experiencing financial freedom and regaining your financial kingdom stewardship. I can't tell you the exact details of that plan because His ways are higher than our ways and His thoughts are higher than our thoughts. In addition, His specific plan varies from person to person. But what I can tell you is that if you will put Him and His principles first in your life, He will show you His plan for you. He will put a thought in your mind that you never had before, or bring some concept to you that shows you how to turn your financial losses into financial gain.

As the poor, in-debt widow discovered when she obeyed God's word given to her by the prophet, He is a debt-cancelling God (2 Kings 4:1-7). God has a way of cancelling out our debts and turning situations around. But you will never discover His plan for you until you seek Him first. "Seek first His kingdom and His righteousness, and all these things will be added to you" (Matthew 6:33).

It's a promise—a promise you can take all the way to the bank.

12

RECLAIMING

We are all concerned about theft. One young mom told me recently that she stayed up while the power was out in her home because the alarm system wouldn't work without power. She wanted to be on alert in case anyone tried to break in. People stealing from us is a real threat. That's why most houses have some form of security system. We have locks on the doors and other preventive measures in place to ward off theft.

Theft is essentially an unauthorized intrusion into our world, home, identity, or surroundings in order to take from us what is rightfully ours. When you travel to highly populated regions, there are often warnings about high-theft areas and tips on how to keep pickpockets at bay. Theft is a reality we have to guard against.

Yet just as people can steal from us in the physical realm, Satan and his demons can steal from us in the spiritual realm. God has already determined and bequeathed to you in your time, talents, and treasures what is yours to rightfully have. But Satan has gone rogue on us by entering our space and stealing from us that which God has already given.

For many of us, he has stolen our joy. For others, he has stolen their peace. And yet for others, he has stolen their dreams, relationships, and dignity. Satan regularly seeks to disrupt the harmony in the home in order to steal the stability of our emotions. He has also slammed doors shut, illegitimately, in far too many people's faces in order to steal their opportunities from them.

Perhaps some of these are ringing a bell with you. Maybe it's that Satan has stolen your purpose. You're here on earth; you just don't know why you are here. You have no sense of a divine calling on your life so you simply meander from day to day, week to week, year to year, and decade to decade. Or maybe purpose is not what's been stolen from you. It could be that it is your health. You may have experienced a setback in your physical or emotional well-being, perhaps not because of something you have done wrong but because of something wrongfully or illegitimately placed on you, or that you have been exposed to.

If none of that sounds familiar to you, consider your assets. For some people, Satan has stolen the fullness of the prosperity intended for them by God. Satan has maneuvered them out of financial blessings God wanted them to have. But now, instead, they are bound in debt so tightly that they can't enjoy what God has for them to enjoy. For others, Satan has maneuvered them away from the kingdom purpose of their financial success. He tricks them into hoarding and only using their assets for themselves.

Satan is a master thief. This isn't his first rodeo. He knows how to rob, kill, steal, and destroy—and he takes pleasure in doing just that.

And if that is not you either, you may want to give thought to your identity. Because stealing people's identity is Satan's number one target of attack. When someone lives with a stolen identity, they no longer know who they are. They wrestle with their gender, value, meaning, significance, and even their hope. In essence, stealing a person's identity can lead to actually stealing a person's life. This brings about a feeling that death is better than life, and they just want to give up trying. When this happens, people may look for illegitimate ways of coping in the midst of being consumed by a painful life. Some people may even take their own lives.

Satan is a master thief. This isn't his first rodeo. He knows how to rob, kill, steal, and destroy (John 10:10)—and he takes pleasure in doing just that. But when you choose to live your life as a kingdom steward, you get one of the greatest benefits available to humanity. You get the ability to get back what the enemy has stolen. You can recover lost goods, lost hope, lost health, lost relationships, lost dreams, lost opportunities, lost identity, and so much more. Friend, whatever Satan has stolen from you, as a kingdom steward under the Lordship of Jesus Christ you have the right to reclaim it.

This is good news for anyone who has been ripped off by the devil or by any of his minions, whether demonic or human. I want you to know beyond a shadow of a doubt that if this is you, you can reclaim the entirety of your stewardship under God. The biblical text we are going to look at which supports this reality is found in 1 Samuel 30. It's a long chapter and I want to encourage you to read it on your own. The summary of the story is that David had come from a battle only to discover that the Amalekites had raided the Negev and burned it with fire. They had taken captive the women and children, along with the spoils in the land. An enormous theft had occurred whereby even David lost his own family members as well. On top of that, they had stolen the cattle and the things they had which contributed to their livelihood. The bottom line is that the thieves had raided and stolen everything of value. So much so, that the Israelites contemplated stoning David and killing him. Their hearts were so deeply saddened and grieved over all they had lost that they blamed their leader and wanted him dead. Scripture tells us they lifted up their voices and wept until there was no more strength in them to weep. Now, keep in mind, these are grown men crying an extreme ugly cry.

Maybe you can relate. Maybe you can understand what would compel them to cry like that. Have you ever cried so hard that you literally ran out of tears to cry? Have you ever wept so long that your tear ducts dried up? The extreme pain and certainty of loss will do that to anyone. When the enemy comes in and rips off those things, hopes, and people we value most in an effort to destroy us, it affects our emotional well-being and stability. There are times in most people's lives when our emotions overtake us because the pain is so great. In those moments, tears flow and words fly—words that may be regretted later. But that's what great loss will do to most anyone. Especially when something has been illegitimately stolen from you.

> *When the enemy comes in and rips off those things, hopes, and people we value most in an effort to destroy us, it affects our emotional well-being and stability.*

It is important to note that David and his men were in enemy territory. This gave the enemy easy access to what legitimately belonged to God's people. It is also important to observe that Satan attacked when the men were absent. Whenever men abandon their spiritual position, they open the door for Satan just like Adam did when his spiritual absence allowed Satan to confiscate everything that had been entrusted to him as a kingdom steward.

First Peter 5:8 reminds us that the devil actively seeks for opportunities to steal from and destroy us. It says, "Be of sober spirit, be on the alert. Your adversary, the devil, prowls around like a roaring lion, seeking someone to devour." And in Ephesians 4:27, we are warned not to give the devil an opportunity. We are to be like the young mom who stayed up during the power outage to make sure no one broke in. We are to be mindful not to leave a window unhooked or a door unlocked. You don't have to welcome the devil in for him to come in. No, all you've got to do is leave him an opportunity to break in. And the way you do that is by coming out from under the alignment of Jesus Christ as Lord of your life. The moment you start acting like the owner of your time, talents, and treasures—rather than the manager—is the moment you have set yourself up for Satan to steal what you have. Because Satan knows just as well as God knows that God will not support, protect, or expand your resources when you are acting as an owner over what rightfully belongs to Him.

When David found himself emotionally distraught from his own loss as well as the loss of those around him, he strengthened himself in the Lord his God.

As we have seen throughout our time together, at the heart of kingdom stewardship is the overarching principle that God owns it all. You and I own nothing. We are merely managers of what He's given us to steward on His behalf. Once you and I begin acting as if we are the owners, we have left a window or door open for the enemy to wreak havoc in our lives. Sin opens the slot for Satan to slide in through.

But once Satan has gotten in and taken off with all the goods, what do you and I do then? After he lost everything to the Amalekites, David showed us what our next step should be.

> Moreover David was greatly distressed because the people spoke of stoning him, for all the people were embittered, each one because of his sons and his daughters. But David strengthened himself in the LORD his God.
>
> I SAMUEL 30:6

Let's start by looking at what David didn't do. For starters, he didn't strengthen himself with alcohol or drugs. Nor did he strengthen himself with an illegitimate relationship or wrong entertainment. When David found himself emotionally distraught from his own loss as well as the loss of those around him, he strengthened himself in the Lord his God. The book of Psalms, many of which were written by David, gives us insight into how this is done. For example, Psalm 42 tells us about a time when David got so depressed that he despaired of all things. He lost all hope. But despite his emotional and physical turmoil he found himself in, David repeatedly returns to the Lord in order to find strength:

> Why are you in despair, O my soul? And why have you become
> disturbed within me? Hope in God, for I shall again praise Him
> for the help of His presence.
>
> PSALM 42:5

> Why are you in despair, O my soul? And why have you become
> disturbed within me? Hope in God, for I shall yet praise Him,
> the help of my countenance and my God.
>
> PSALM 42:11

David instructed himself to place his hope in God. Even though he couldn't see the positive outcome to the situation that stared him down, he reminded himself of the help of God's presence. He practiced the presence of God while simultaneously surrendering to the current situation. David was able to do that because he had witnessed God's provision and protection in the past and knew that he could count on Him for the future.

David reminds us of this mindset we should all have throughout many of the psalms, including Psalm 34 where he writes,

> I sought the LORD, and He answered me, and delivered me from
> all my fears. They looked to Him and were radiant, and their

faces will never be ashamed. This poor man cried, and the LORD heard him and saved him out of all his troubles. The angel of the LORD encamps around those who fear Him, and rescues them.

PSALM 34:4-7

Also, in Psalm 23 David reminds himself that God is the great Shepherd who leads him beside the calm waters. Time and time again, David stewarded his emotions by directing his thoughts back to the faithfulness and sovereignty of God. He even did this when he needed to address sin in his own life (Psalms 32, 38, and 51). Living with a divine perspective enabled David to find strength in those times when most people would have simply given up. After all, his own people threatened to stone him for the losses they were experiencing. He had guilt on top of fear on top of personal pain to contend with. That's a lot for anyone, let alone a man leading a nation in a time of grief. But David was wise enough to know that he could not move forward in his own strength. He had to rely on God, so he did what had become his habit of doing—he strengthened himself in the Lord his God.

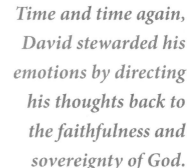

Time and time again, David stewarded his emotions by directing his thoughts back to the faithfulness and sovereignty of God.

That's the first thing David did. But the second thing he did gives us even greater insight into how we can likewise go about reclaiming the stewardship the enemy has stolen. In 1 Samuel 30:7-8, we read that David sought spiritual counsel. He knew he could not fight this battle alone so he invited the wisdom of the priest. He asked for help and guidance from God. It says,

Then David said to Abiathar the priest, the son of Ahimelech, "Please bring me the ephod." So Abiathar brought the ephod to David. David inquired of the LORD, saying, "Shall I pursue this band? Shall I overtake them?"

David didn't go to his bank first. Nor did he go to his legal authorities or professional counselors. Rather, he went to the priest because the priest had the ephod, which was the official garment the priest would wear when he entered into the presence of God. On the ephod was a breastplate over the chest and attached to this breastplate was what is called the Urim and Thummim. These were like two stones attached to the pouch and were used to get guidance from God. Essentially, David used the spiritual tools and weapons available to him at that time in order to seek God's will and guidance on what he was supposed to do regarding what had been stolen from them as a nation.

We can all learn a lesson from David's action. He went to the priest in order to inquire of God himself. There's only so much a priest can do, and David was aware of that. So he asked to have the items that would usher him into God's presence more fully for guidance.

But we do need to go to God and ask Him for the wisdom and guidance to apply to our specific scenario.

Sometimes people expect other people, because of their positions, to speak to them on God's behalf. They want to know God's solution to their situation but they look to someone else to deliver that answer. Through His Son Jesus Christ, God has given each of us access to His throne directly. We don't need the ephod to enter because God has given us the Holy Spirit. But we do need to go to God and ask Him for the wisdom and guidance to apply to our specific scenario. Rather than rushing forward with our own plan of attack, David's example reminds us to start by gaining strength in the Lord first and then going to God for wisdom on what to do next.

All believers have every right to both seek and get personal guidance in the specific situation they are facing because of the anointing they received in Christ (1 John 2:20, 27). This anointing "teaches you" and shows you the way to proceed. Let me remind you that the job of pastors and spiritual teachers on the Internet or in books and studies is to encourage you in your growth. Their job is not to tell you where God wants you to go and what God wants you to do. That role belongs to God Himself. Never confuse spiritual gifts in people with God. Gifts are good and useful

> *The primary way you are to look to God is through His Word.*

for the building up of the saints but only God knows the full plan, from the beginning to the end, of how He wants to use your life for His glory. Look to Him.

The primary way you are to look to God is through His Word. The Word of God is comprised of three variations. There is the Graphe, which refers to that which has been recorded and written down. The Graphe is the Bible that we carry to church, read in our homes, or read through a Bible app. The second variation is the Logos, which is the content and the meaning of what was recorded. The third variation is what is known as the Rhema, which has to do with the application of the specific Word to your own situation.

The Graphe is simply the writing in the Bible. The Logos is the understanding and the meaning of the Bible. But the Rhema is where the Holy Spirit lifts the words off the page and applies it to your specific scenario. It is also known as the anointing. Thus, when a person comes to church carrying a Bible, they are carrying the Graphe. When they hear a pastor preach, they are hearing the Logos. But in order to apply the meaning to their own lives, that takes the work of the Spirit by providing the Rhema.

I like to explain it by using football. In football, the NFL has an overarching rule book. The rule book applies to all thirty-two teams. Each team's coach and all the players must abide by the same exact rule book. But not all thirty-two teams have the same playbook. The playbook differs from team to team and even from situation to situation. This is because each individual team has its own strategies, goals, and situations.

Similarly, all of us are to live our lives underneath the governance of God's Graphe and Logos, His revealed Word and its meaning. But God has a unique playbook for each person. He has one with your name on it. When you are in touch with the Holy Spirit through abiding with Jesus as Lord of your life, consistent with the rule book of God's Word, you gain access to God's playbook (His Rhema word) for your personal life.

Not only that, if you have ever watched football at all, then you know that sometimes a quarterback will "call an audible" on the line of scrimmage. This happens when he looks out and sees that the defense is doing something different than he expected. He can tell by the way they are lined up that the previously chosen play isn't going to work all that well, so he chooses another play right there on the spot. When he calls an audible, the entire team starts shifting and moving because the play has changed.

If you are not closely in touch with God, you won't hear Him when He calls an audible in your life. Neither will you be able to recognize the changes in the defense—the enemy—and, as a result, you may wind up running the same old play in each and every situation of life. Reclaiming what the enemy has stolen requires you to be in constant close proximity to God so that His guidance is what moves you and guides your actions.

David needed to hear from God. He didn't know who had stolen from him, the entirety of what had been stolen, or where it had been taken. He was without direction and didn't know what to do next. Maybe David's situation is sounding all too familiar to you right now. Maybe you are in a situation where you don't know what to do. You don't know how to repair the circumstances. You don't know how to get back what you have lost. In fact, you may feel so aimless in what to do that throwing in the towel is the best option that comes to mind. But before you actually throw in that towel, I want to remind you of your access to God. When you seek Him and His specific direction for your situation in life, He will give you insight into how to get back the stewardship you have lost.

David started out in his inquiry of God by asking Him if he should pursue the enemy. He had a specific question that he wanted God to answer. As we read in verse 1 Samuel 30:8, "Shall I pursue this band? Shall I overtake them?" God's response to David came back quickly. He said, "Pursue, for you will surely overtake them, and you will surely rescue all."

David received a Rhema word, which applied to his specific situation. In it, God told David to do something. Often, God is asking us to do something. A person shouldn't ask God for a job and then just sit there rather than go job-hunting. God wants to see you walk by faith with the little He has revealed to you before He is going to give you more information. Far too many people are waiting on God to reclaim what they have lost, but God is waiting on them to do what He has asked them to do. Because David was willing to do as God said, he positioned himself to retrieve what the enemy had stolen. David knew God had his back.

When Christians seek God's power but do not find it, it is often a result of this lack of communication with God.

What's more, David stayed in close communication with God. Similar to how a cell phone must be charged in order to have enough power to function, staying connected to God—abiding in Jesus—gives us the power we need to carry out His instructions. When Christians seek God's power but do not find it, it is often a result of this lack of communication with God. Sure, they may wonder why the Holy Spirit is not speaking. Or they may wonder why the anointing isn't working. They may even wonder where the loot is that the enemy took from their lives. But unless you make a concerted effort to operate in high communication with the One who knows all, you will limit your access to God's power and wisdom. Knowing God is fundamental to knowing His will and purposes for you.

Once David heard from God, and God confirmed the plan of action he was to take, David was able to head out to recover what had been taken. He moved in faith to retrieve what the enemy had stolen. Remember, God's promises are within your reach, and moving in faith places them in your hand. On the way to the location, though, we read that David and his men ran into a wandering Egyptian.

> Now they found an Egyptian in the field and brought him to
> David, and gave him bread and he ate, and they provided him
> water to drink. They gave him a piece of fig cake and two clusters
> of raisins, and he ate; then his spirit revived. For he had not eaten
> bread or drunk water for three days and three nights.
>
> I SAMUEL 30:11-12

After the Egyptian had eaten and regained his strength, David asked him who he was and whom he belonged to. That's when the Egyptian shared that he belonged to the group of people who had made a raid on the Israelites just a few days earlier. He had fallen sick, and they had left him behind to die (verses 13-15).

God had honored David's obedience by bringing a scout along the path for him to run into. This starving, sick man had no other choice but to receive the food and give the information to David and his men. Friend,

God knows how to intersect your pathways with the right person at the right time in order to usher you into the right location He has for you.

David further inquired of the man if he knew where the rest of his people had gone. Once the Egyptian was assured that his life would be spared, he then let them know exactly where they had gone and what they had planned to do. He also told David that he would take them directly to the people, which he did.

When David and his men had originally set out to retrieve what had been taken from them, no one would have been able to guess the strategy God used to get them to the exact location they needed to go. That's why staying close in communication with God is so critical. You've got to move with God and not try to predict Him. God can never be put in a box because He will use some of the most unlikely people and unusual means in His divine providence to turn your situation around.

What you need to remember is that God knows right where your stuff is. He knows where the enemy has taken it, and He knows what the enemy is trying to do with it. Satan wants to use the stewardship he steals from God's people in order to advance his own kingdom.

David continued to move in faith and followed the Egyptian to where he said he would take him. When he did, David and his men found those who had previously raided their land dancing and drinking in celebration of their great victory. They were in no position to defend themselves. They were too busy having a party with somebody else's stuff.

But David outsmarted them because he attacked them at their greatest vulnerability. Scripture tells us that not a man escaped, other than the four hundred young men who fled on camels. David successfully recovered all that the Amalekites had taken and nothing that had been stolen was missing. David brought it all back: the women, children, sheep, cattle, possessions—everything. He got it back, all because his men were willing to feed a starving man who had been left for dead. That reminds me of

Hebrews 13:2, "Do not neglect to show hospitality to strangers, for by this some have entertained angels without knowing it."

God knows how to preserve your stolen stewardship. God has solutions for you that you will never be able to guess are solutions. It's up to you to be obedient throughout the process. Reclaiming your stewardship also involves engaging in spiritual warfare. David had to be willing to fight for it. But it is also key to remember that God has already given us the victory in spiritual warfare (1 John 5:4; Revelation 12:11).

Not only did David get back what had been stolen from the Israelites, though. The good news is he got more than that. The Amalekites had raided several lands. Their loot came from many places. God can not only preserve your stuff and help you get it back, but He can also give you that which has been stored up for others as well, which goes to show just how great God is. Proverbs 13:22 says, "The wealth of the sinner is stored up for the righteous."

Friend, the enemy has been defeated. God knows exactly how you are to get back what he has stolen.

God is able to do more than you could ever imagine. Second Corinthians 2:14 puts it this way: "But thanks be to God, who always leads us in triumph in Christ, and manifests through us the sweet aroma of the knowledge of Him in every place." And Romans 8:37 says it like this: "But in all these things we overwhelmingly conquer through Him who loved us."

Friend, the enemy has been defeated. God knows exactly how you are to get back what he has stolen. Colossians 2:15 reminds us of this reality: "When He had disarmed the rulers and authorities, He made a public display of them, having triumphed over them through Him." Satan has no right to your stuff. But you will allow him to keep it if you do not choose to go after it God's way. While God does not always restore, heal, or return what you have lost—if it's His will to do so, you can pursue that by aligning yourself under Him. You can get back your joy. You can get back your peace. You can get back your family, career, stability, identity, health, and so much more. You can get it all back, if God wills, because the devil is a defeated foe. As the manager assigned to steward the time, talents, and treasures God has given to you, it belongs to you. You must go and get back what the enemy has stolen.

You may have heard the story of "Jack and the Beanstalk" when you were growing up, or perhaps you've read it to your kids or grandkids. In one of the versions of this English fairy tale, Jack lives with his mom in a cottage just outside of London. The little garden they own is no longer producing food, and the cow's milk has become weak. The mom convinces Jack that the only way they will survive is for him to sell the cow. So Jack goes to sell the cow to the butcher. But on the way to the butcher, he comes across an elderly man. The elderly man offers him three magic beans in exchange for the cow. The elderly man convinces Jack that if the three magic beans don't work, he can buy back his cow.

Believing the man's claims, Jack exchanges the cow for the three beans. But when Jack gets home and tells his mom what he did, she doesn't share his perspective. In fact, Mama is mad. She takes the three beans from Jack's hand and throws them out the window and sends Jack to bed without his supper.

The next morning when Jack wakes up, there is a beanstalk growing outside of their cottage. The beanstalk stretches all the way into the heavens. The magic beans were magic after all. So Jack climbs the beanstalk, and when he gets to the top he discovers a castle. During his exploration of the castle, Jack learns that the castle used to belong to his father but a giant had killed his father and stolen the castle. Jack learns that everything in that castle is rightfully his. You know the story. Jack then waits for the giant to fall asleep and when he does, Jack picks up a basket holding a hen that lays golden eggs and makes his way back to the beanstalk.

But all that movement wakes the giant so the giant pursues him yelling, "Fee! Fie! Fo! Fum! I smell the blood of an Englishman. Be he alive or be he dead, I will grind his bones to make my bread." The giant takes off after Jack but Jack is too fast. As the giant chases him down the stalk, Jack reaches the bottom faster and cuts the stalk until it falls over. The giant falls to his death and Jack reclaims what has been bequeathed to him by his father.

What I want you to know from this children's story is that there is another tree that connects heaven and earth. This tree is a bridge between glory and history, between heaven and earth. Jesus tells us about this tree in John 15:1 where He says He is the true vine. If you will abide in Him, know Him, and go where He directs you to go, Jesus can take you to the location where Satan has stored your loot under lock and key. Jesus knows right where you should go. But you will need to make Him the central point of all you think, say, and do.

Once you reclaim what God has bequeathed to you through His Son, you can say your own rhyme of sorts, "Fee! Fie! Fo! Fum! I have the blood of God's only begotten Son. He is alive, although He once was dead. And now He is my eternal Bread."

So, inform the devil you are coming now in the name of the Lord Jesus Christ as His kingdom steward and in the power of the Holy Spirit based on God's inerrant Word to get your stuff back. And tell the devil you won't take no for an answer!

Friend, when you connect Jesus Christ to your role of living as a kingdom steward, you will gain access to all God has in store for you, and more. You will get back what the enemy has stolen. Then you can move forward in rightfully managing the time, talents, and treasures He's placed in your care.

CONCLUSION

When you know what I know about your eternal future, and when you know what I know about this world, which is that all of these earthly things will burn, it changes your perspective. Sinners don't know what I know. They think that this life holds all there is. They don't know that God takes into account what you do in time for eternity. If you are a Christian, and if you know what I know, no investment for heaven should be too much. What you do in time will determine what you experience in glory.

Now that you have the pivotal understanding of kingdom stewardship, you should be motivated to devote yourself daily to living as a kingdom steward. Keep this definition of kingdom stewardship with you as you go throughout your days: Kingdom stewardship is the divinely authorized responsibility for believers to faithfully oversee the protection and expansion of the assets (time, talents, and treasures) that God has entrusted to them to manage on His behalf.

Always keep at the forefront of your thoughts the truth that all you have been given belongs to the Giver. God's desire is that you will serve Him enthusiastically and that you will honor Him as Lord over your life. By committing to using the time, talents, and treasures He provides, you will also better position yourself to receive great rewards.

Let your every word and action pass through the filter of His ownership first. Use your time wisely because the days pass by quickly. God wants to reward you, but He won't force you to obey Him. That is up to you. You can start by aligning your thoughts each morning when you wake up by acknowledging God's ownership over every area of your life. A sample prayer might go like this:

Lord, You gave me life. You gave me today. I thank You for it, and I turn this day over to You. Have Your way in my thoughts. Have Your way in my time. Have Your way in my talents. Have Your way in my dreams. Have Your way in my work. Have your way in the use of the resources You have entrusted to me. Have Your way with my words. Have Your way with my relationships. Lord, everything about this day, I hand over to You. Guide me because You own me. I place myself in Your hands. In Jesus' name, amen.

I would encourage you to follow up that prayer by meditating on and saying Galatians 2:20, "I have been crucified with Christ; and it is no longer I who live, but Christ lives in me; and the life which I now live in the flesh I live by faith in the Son of God, who loved me and gave Himself up for me."

I want to challenge you to begin each day with a prayer like this and to focus on God's Word. Start your day by remembering what your day is all about: God. Invite Him into your thoughts and actions. Invite His rule to reign over you. Let Him influence what you do, who you do it with, what you watch, how you spend your time, and what you say. That's the true definition of stewardship. If it were only about money, it would be easy. But stewardship has to do with every single area of your life, even your thoughts.

When God governs you and you live as a wise manager investing and leveraging all He's given to you in order to advance and promote the agenda of His kingdom, you will be living as a faithful kingdom steward. You will also be taking full advantage of His incentive clauses and rewards program in your life.

Get up each day and affirm God's ownership along with your commitment to serve as His faithful manager to impact your life for His glory, your good, the benefit of others, and the advancement of His kingdom. Remember, your life is like a coin. You can spend it any way you wish, but you only get to spend it once. God bless you richly as you steward this life in light of the life that is to come.

ACKNOWLEDGMENTS

I want to thank my friends at Focus on the Family and Tyndale House Publishers for their long-standing partnership in bringing my thoughts, study, and words to print. I particularly want to thank Larry Weeden for his friendship over the years, as well as his pursuit of excellence in the Kingdom line of books and materials. I also want to publicly thank Steve Johnson, Allison Montjoy, Beth Robinson, and Whitney Harrison for their work in getting this book into the marketplace. In addition, my appreciation goes out to Heather Hair for her skills and insights in collaboration on this manuscript.

NOTES

Chapter 1: Meaning

1. Camille Preston, "How Organizations Can Help Employees Self-Manage," *Forbes*, August 25, 2017, https://www.forbes.com/sites/forbescoachescouncil/2017/08/25/how -organizations-can-help-employees-self-manage/#75d13f6614b9.

Chapter 2: Mindset

1. Joe Pinsker, "'Ugh, I'm So Busy': A Status Symbol for Our Time," *The Atlantic*, March 1, 2017, https://www.theatlantic.com/business/archive/2017/03/busyness-status-symbol /518178/.

Chapter 3: Motivation

1. Max Lucado (@MaxLucado), Instagram, January 24, 2019.

Chapter 9: Profession

1. "Workplace Stress," The American Institute of Stress, accessed August 8, 2019, https:// www.stress.org/workplace-stress.

Chapter 10: Rewards

1. *The Daily Wire*, "Dave Ramsey: The Ben Shapiro Show Sunday Special, Episode 36," *YouTube* video, 59:24, February 3, 2019, https://youtube.com/watch?v=l-Kdq8cET1g.

Chapter 11: Release

1. Sarah O'Brien, "Fed Survey Shows 40 Percent of Adults Still Can't Cover a $400 Emergency Expense," *CNBC*, May 22, 2018, https://www.cnbc.com/2018/05/22/fed-survey-40-percent -of-adults-cant-cover-400-emergency-expense.html.
2. "100 Million Dieters, $20 Billion: The Weight-Loss Industry by the Numbers," *ABC News*, May 8, 2012, https://abcnews.go.com/Health/100-million-dieters-20-billion -weight-loss-industry/story?id=16297197.

TonyEVANS
THE URBAN ALTERNATIVE

YOUR *Eternity* IS OUR *Priority*

At The Urban Alternative, eternity is our priority—for the individual, the family, the church and the nation. The 45-year teaching ministry of Tony Evans has allowed us to reach a world in need with:

The Alternative – Our flagship radio program brings hope and comfort to an audience of millions on over 1,400 radio outlets across the country.

tonyevans.org – Our library of teaching resources provides solid Bible teaching through the inspirational books and sermons of Tony Evans.

Tony Evans Training Center – Experience the adventure of God's Word with our online classroom, providing at-your-own-pace courses for your PC or mobile device.

Tony Evans app – Packed with audio and video clips, devotionals, Scripture readings and dozens of other tools, the mobile app provides inspiration on-the-go.

Explore God's kingdom today.
Live for more than the moment.
Live for *eternity*.

tonyevans.org

CP1507

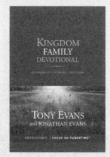

THE KINGDOM SERIES
FROM DR. TONY EVANS